IQ MAY GET YOU
A JOB;
EQ GETS YOU
PROMOTED

IQ MAY GET YOU A JOB; EQ GETS YOU PROMOTED

Gilles Azzopardi

foulsham
LONDON • NEW YORK • TORONTO • SYDNEY

foulsham

The Publishing House, Bennetts Close,
Cippenham, Berkshire, SL1 5AP, England.

ISBN 0-572-02584-X

This English language edition © 2001 W. Foulsham & Co. Ltd
Originally published by Marabout (Belgique) © 1998 under the
title *QE, QI Dopez Votre Intelligence*.

Cover photograph © The Stock Market / Jon Feingersh

Printed in Great Britain by Bath Press, Bath

CONTENTS

CHAPTER ONE

THE TWO FORMS OF INTELLIGENCE

'Intelligence is a mental aptitude that involves, amongst other things, the abilities of reasoning, anticipation, resolving problems, abstract thinking, understanding complex ideas, rapid thinking and gaining from experience.

'It is not only an academic ability or an aptitude for tests. It reflects an enhanced ability to understand our environment, to seize opportunities, to make sense of things and to think up practical solutions. Thus defined, intelligence may be measured, and IQ tests measure it well.'

This definition of intelligence introduced the *Wall Street Journal* manifesto and it is, without a doubt, the most complete definition to date. It corresponds quite well to the general consensus amongst psychologists, neurophysiologists, anthropologists and other intelligence professionals. Furthermore, it reveals a new approach, suggesting that intelligence cannot be defined only according to strict rational criteria, as has been done since the start of the century.

RATIONAL INTELLIGENCE AND EMOTIONAL INTELLIGENCE

The difference is in the words 'amongst other things'; this short phrase opens up the whole meaning of intelligence, no longer restricting it to verbal and logical mathematical capacities. There is not just one type of intelligence that everybody values, but two.

On the one hand, we have rational intelligence, which backs up our mental functions. On the other, emotional intelligence is responsible for our sensitivity – which explains why girls are more efficient at all stages of life than boys, why some people happily climb the ladder of success while others remain for ever on the bottom rung. Or why there are idiots who make a fortune whilst a lot of intelligent people find it difficult to make both ends meet, and why some couples argue and separate yet some couples who argue stay together.

Your thoughts are governed by your emotions and so, frequently, are your decisions.

THE EMOTIONAL QUOTIENT

It is widely believed today that intelligence is reason; that we act with logic. But this is not the case.

We go by instinct, we decide by using our feelings and all the more so when we are being persuaded to the contrary. Whatever the level of our IQ, we still have the intelligence of our emotions first and foremost.

And so the real measure of intelligence is not only our intelligence quotient – our IQ – but also our emotional quotient, or EQ. A high EQ is characterised by the ability to read the feelings of others, to put ourselves in their shoes; and by self-control – the ability to control our impulses, to reason and to remain calm in all circumstances, and to be optimistic despite difficulties and hardships.

The twentieth century has been a time of great revolution, when feelings and emotions have finally triumphed over the technical experts. We are now seeing the end of merciless planning and management based on juggled figures and statistics, and of decisions taken by faceless authority. In the future, the true values will be intuition, gentleness, sympathy, discussion and compliance. It is through these that problems will be solved. The future lies with those who have a high EQ.

THE EQ IN AMERICA

In America, a high intelligence quotient has always been what matters: it is the key to success (possibly after belief in God). IQ decides everything from kindergarten and university entrance to job possibilities and career moves.

Those with a low IQ are relegated to schools in the lowest category, stuck in jobs without prospects and bluntly excluded from the system, socially speaking. In the 1950s, IQ measurement was even the basis for strongly racist theses. William Schrockley, winner of a Nobel Prize for physics and inventor of the transistor, put forward a proposal that all black Americans should be sterilised – on the grounds that they achieved poor results in IQ tests that had taken place on a vast scale in several Southern States.

Today, though, the importance of IQ in the United States is diminishing. Although in some schools children are still selected by their IQ, the curriculum now offers lessons in emotional education in order to fight against adolescent aggression and violence. It has actually been found that emotional education is more effective in reducing the numbers of unwanted pregnancies than sex education.

EQ, THE NEW KEY TO SUCCESS

In business, EQ is making great strides. The fashionable slogan is 'IQ gets you hired but EQ gets you promoted'. EQ is fast becoming the new key to success.

Bell Labs, the high technology research centre for AT&T, the giant telecom power in the USA, asked Daniel Goleman, a psychologist at Harvard, to test his brightest students. The best results were not from those with the highest IQ or the most prestigious diplomas. 'On the contrary,' concluded Gorman, 'The stars were those whose personal qualities put them in the centre of the communication networks which they created themselves in moments of crisis or innovation. When they encountered a problem and asked for help, they got it immediately.' The others, it turned out, had to wait several days to get a response.

A study carried out in America and Europe by the Centre for Creative Leadership, to understand why so many young people apparently destined for a shining future go off the rails, reached the same conclusions: their failure was due to a disastrously low EQ – an inability to communicate with others. When you experience failure in your job, it seems, it's more likely to be due to emotional problems than a lack of competence.

Metlife, the insurance company, has taken lessons from this. They used to hire 5,000 sales reps a year. Each recruit cost them thousands of pounds in training. Half dropped out at the end of a year and four out of five left within four years. To put an end to this dramatic loss of manpower, Metlife entrusted Martin Seligman, a psychologist at the University of Pennsylvania, with the task of recruiting 15,000 sales reps.

Seligman used two tests: one group took the IQ test usually applied by Metlife and the other took an EQ test created by Seligman himself. In the group recruited by Seligman's EQ method, turnover was 21 per cent lower at the end of the first year than the group recruited in the usual way and 57 per cent lower at the end of the second year.

In Europe we are still lagging behind, however. IQ tests are still often used to move students into the second year of a course, to select recruits for the armed forces or for entrance to certain companies. But this won't always be the criterion. We now know that cool, detached, objective intelligence is rarely enough: it is those well-rounded, sympathetic, optimistic individuals who are the most successful.

Success, then, seems to lie not only in the domain of rational intelligence, but also in that of emotional intelligence. And through understanding of this, my book will help you to develop your full potential and find your own key to success.

CHAPTER 2

RATIONAL INTELLIGENCE

In its strictest sense, intelligence represents the mental functions necessary for conceptual and rational recognition. It distinguishes between feelings and intuition. Most experts group the different forms of intelligence in pairs: sensory–motor/rational; abstract/concrete; theoretical/practical; logical/empirical.

Our **sensory–motor intelligence** is developed in early infancy. It is during this time that we learn to deal with the practical problems posed by our environment. Our level of sensory–motor intelligence depends very much upon our family circumstances and our social and cultural surroundings. Given a rich diversity of situations, stimuli and experiences, our development will be at its optimum level. Equally, if our immediate surroundings are dull and impoverished, then our development will be similarly disadvantaged.

Once adolescence and then adulthood have been reached, the development of our sensory–motor intelligence is virtually nil.

In our modern society, **rational intelligence** takes precedence over sensory–motor intelligence. The modern man compares to primitive man in much the same way as an adult does to a child. Primitive man discovered the basic techniques and modern man, through great inventions, has developed them to utilise them in a more advanced way.

Nowadays, the term 'intelligence' refers primarily to understanding, reason and even communication, rather than practical experience.

The observation of sensory–motor intelligence (which has a concrete, practical aspect) has shown that it brings several abilities into play, including lateral thinking and both making and using appropriate tools. A similar examination of rational intelligence leads us to pose, more directly, the question of the nature of intelligence. Is this a unique faculty suitable for different applications? Or is it made up of different abilities that contribute to the same objective (e.g. solving a problem)? Nowadays, experts are divided over this. Some believe in an overall intelligence, others in a combination of abilities.

OVERALL INTELLIGENCE

The idea of overall intelligence is evidential. We experience and use it every day in our daily routine. When we are occupied with a problem, we are not aware of the different abilities that come into play. Our intellectual function is not separated into different parts for different activities.

Studies on rational intelligence confirm this point. When individuals were given a number of different problems to solve, it was possible to observe and measure a general factor of intelligence common to all.

MIXED INTELLIGENCE

The idea of a composite or mixed intelligence dates back to the end of the nineteeth century. But since then, intelligence has no longer been defined as only a single faculty but as a combination of particular aptitudes. Perception, language and memory are the most fundamental of these, while reasoning, judgement and critical ability are required for more sophisticated functions.

The number of factors brought together in intelligence can vary from nought to 120 and often more, according to the specialists.

FACTORS IN INTELLIGENCE

Nearly all experts in cognitive science agree nevertheless that seven factors in particular contribute to the functioning of rational intelligence.

* **Spatial perception**: the ability to perceive and compare flat and 3D shapes

* **Recognition**: the ability to identify a given shape in a complex layout

* **Memory**: the ability to memorise and reproduce groups without logical relation

* **Reasoning**: the ability to think logically and draw conclusions

* **Numeracy**: the ability to manipulate figures

* **Comprehension**: the ability to understand words

* **Verbalisation**: the ability to use vocabulary

EXERCISING YOUR NEURONES

Above all else, our degree of rational intelligence depends on training. In this respect, intellectual function resembles bodily function. Both our minds and bodies get out of shape if they are not used. Just as we build up our muscles when we work out, so we can increase our intelligence with frequent exercise.

The programme laid out in Chapters 4–8 is designed to stimulate certain mental functions and to enhance your performance in the following fields:

* Logic and reasoning

* Memory

* Language and understanding

✳ Spatial intelligence and perception

In all these fields, the numerical factor plays a particular role. It may be very evident as in the use of logic/memory or it may be underlying as in language/spatial intelligence.

CHAPTER 3

EVALUATING YOUR IQ

This chapter is designed to help you to evaluate your IQ. It is made up of two tests, each containing 20 problems.

At the beginning of each test you will find examples to familiarise you with the types of problems posed.

This evaluation is only valid if you stick to the following rules:

✳ You may only take 15 minutes per test. Once this time is up, don't try to finish or correct your answers.

✳ You can spend time studying the examples and take a break for a couple of minutes between the two tests.

✳ You must solve the problems mentally – do not use calculators or dictionaries.

✳ You must complete both tests before assessing your answers.

A few words of advice ...

✳ You will need just over half an hour to complete BOTH the tests. Make sure that you set aside enough time to do them without being distracted.

✳ You will have less than 1 minute per problem, so you mustn't waste time. If you get stuck on a question, don't spend time thinking about it – move on to the next one.

✳ Make sure you answer as many questions as you can. It is almost impossible to answer them all in the allotted time, so don't worry if you have to leave a few unanswered.

✳ Set an alarm clock or timer before you start each test so you don't have to keep checking the time.

✳ Don't check over your answers in the break between the tests: it will make you doubt what you have written.

✳ Don't guess at answers – you can't calculate your IQ by guesswork.

EXAMPLES

1. Find the missing picture to complete the sequence:

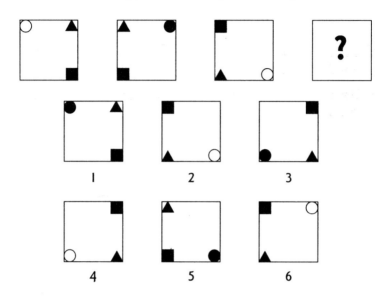

2. Complete the sequence:

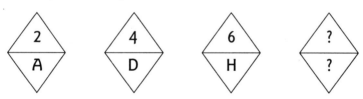

3. Insert the missing number:

4. Insert the missing letter:

A1   D2   I3   _4

5. Insert in the brackets one word that has the same meaning as both the other words:

test (- - -) attempt

6. Find the picture that completes the sequence:

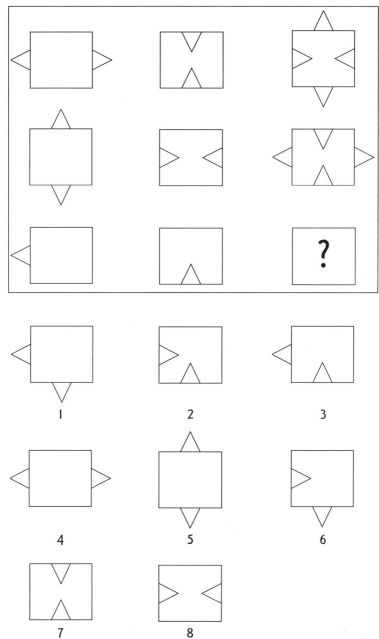

SOLUTIONS

1. Picture 3
The circle and the square rotate clockwise and the circle changes colour each time. The triangle moves anticlockwise.

2.

Add 2 to the number every time: 2 (+2) = 4 (+2) = 6 (+2) = 8

The letters follow an increasing progression
D = third letter after A
H = fourth letter after D
M = fifth letter after H

3. 88
In the second circle, the numbers are those of the first circle divided by 2. In the third circle, they are the first multiplied by 2.

4. P
The position of each letter in the alphabet corresponds with the square of the number that accompanies it.

5. Try

6. Picture 6
On each line, the right-hand picture incorporates the triangles in the same positions as the preceding pictures and inverts them.

TEST 1

NB: You have 15 minutes to solve 20 problems.

1. Find the missing picture to complete the sequence:

   1   2   3

   4   5   6

2. Insert the missing letter:

98 (N)   648 (S)   325 (T)   513 (-)

3. Insert the missing word:

            A2 DI N4 W3   DAWN

            A4 M3 N5 HI U2 -----

4. Using the example to help you, insert the missing word in the brackets:

         spent   (stem)   empty

         frill   (----)   each

5. Find the missing numbers:

I	8	9	64	25	?	49
I	4	27	16	125	?	343

6. Find the picture to complete the sequence:

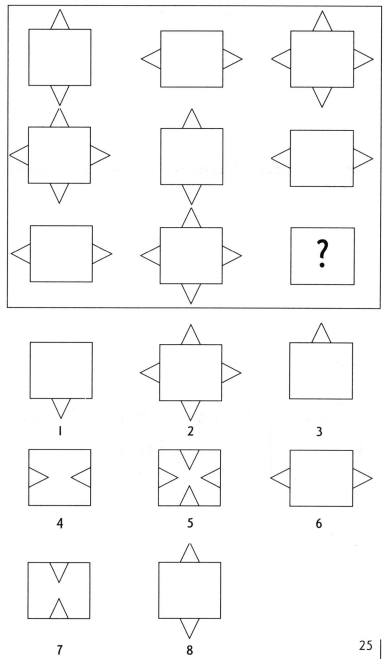

7. Insert the missing number:

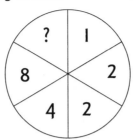

8. Complete the table:

C	H	M
F	J	N
?	L	O

9. Insert the letter to complete the sequence:

A C A E A G A K A M A -

10. Find the picture to complete the sequence:

1   2   3

4   5   6

11. Find the picture to complete the sequence:

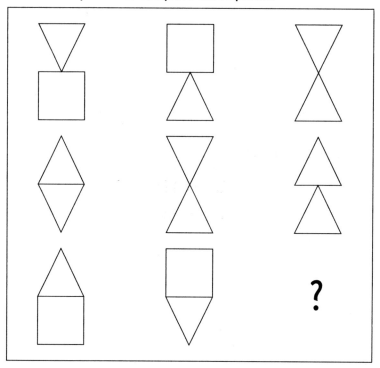

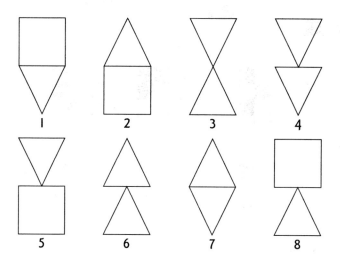

12. Find the picture to complete the sequence:

1   2   3

4   5   6

13. Insert the missing letters:

    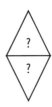

14. Complete the sequence:

  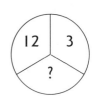

15. Using the example to help you, insert the missing word in the brackets:

coat   (take)   peek

pals   (- - - -)   ride

16. Find the picture to complete the sequence:

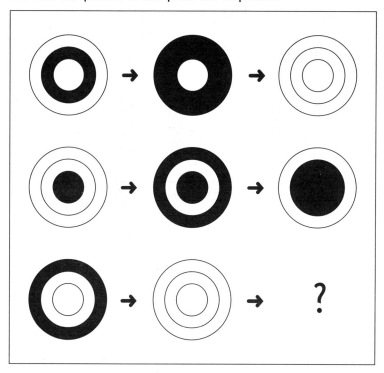

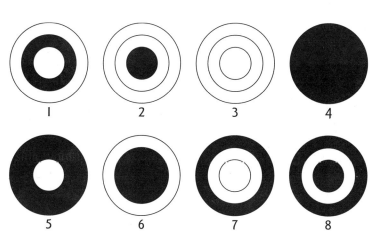

17. Find the picture to complete the sequence:

 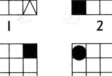 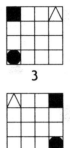

1   2   3

4   5   6

18. Complete the table:

3	12	8
7	28	24
5	20	?

19. Complete the sequence:

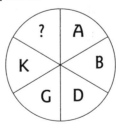

20. Insert one word in the brackets that has the same meaning as the other two words:

narrowboat   (- - - - -)   push

TEST 2

NB: You have 15 minutes to solve 20 problems.

1. Find the picture to complete the sequence:

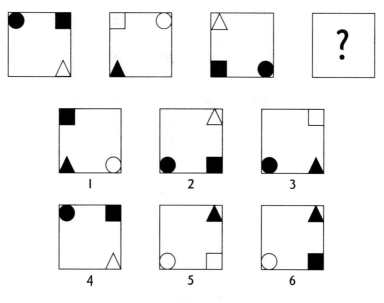

2. Insert the missing number:

IV	3	II	2	XII	4	VIII	5
XVI	5	III	3	V	2	XIX	-

3. Using the example to help you, insert the missing word in the brackets:

marks   (rose)   alone

apple   (- - - -)   shell

4. Insert the missing number:

A 43   C 52   E 61   G 8-

5. Insert the missing number:

326   (20)   432

427   (-)   113

6. Find the picture to complete the sequence:

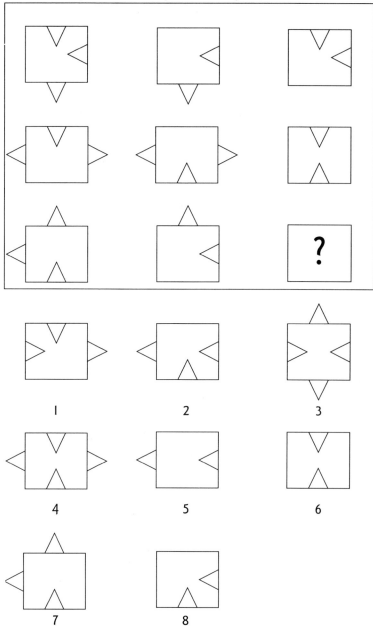

7. Find the picture to complete the sequence:

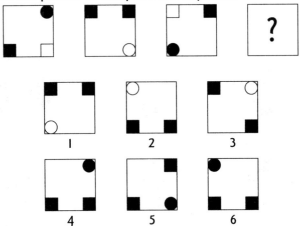

8. Complete the table:

8	4	3	9
5	7	3	9
3	1	2	?

9. Complete the sequence:

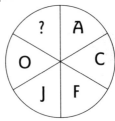

10. Using the example to help you, insert the missing word in the brackets:

kilt   (took)   polo

raid   (- - - -)   cape

11. Find the picture to complete the sequence:

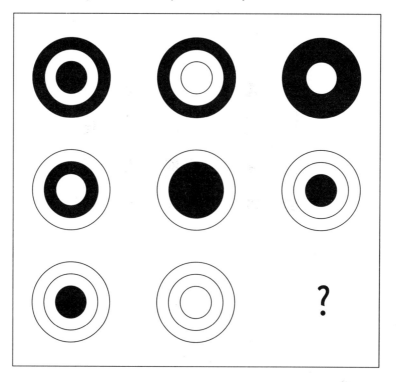

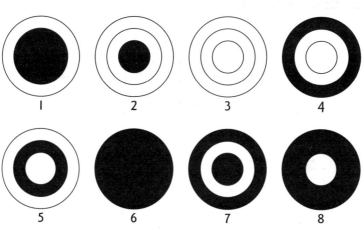

12. Complete the sequence:

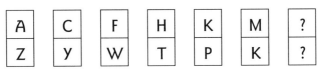

A	C	F	H	K	M	?
Z	Y	W	T	P	K	?

13. Insert the missing number:

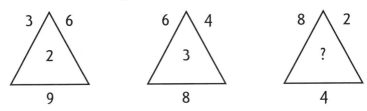

14. Insert one word in the brackets that has the same meaning as the other two words:

pull   (- - - -)   illustrate

15. Find the picture to complete the sequence:

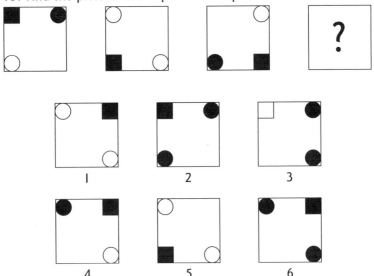

16. Find the picture to complete the sequence:

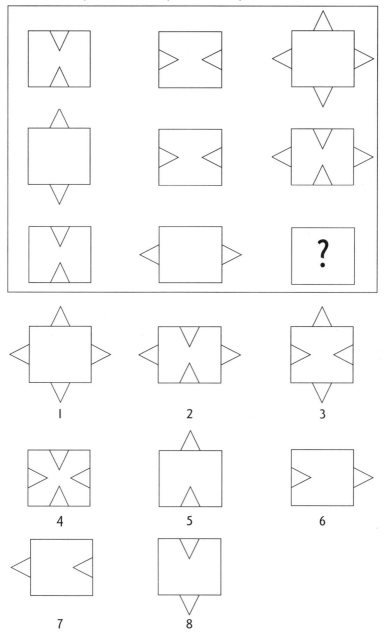

17. Find the picture to complete the sequence:

1 2 3

4 5 6

18. Insert the missing numbers:

19. Complete the sequence:

20. Using the example to help you, insert the correct word in the brackets

cbjm   sfou   qmbz

bail   rent   (- - - -)

SOLUTIONS: TEST 1

1. Picture 2

The two interior lines of the square rotate clockwise each time by 90°.

2. F

The letter following each number is the first letter of the number when it is written as a word.

3. HUMAN

The numbers after the letters give the position of the letters in the word.

4. Flea

To make the word in the brackets, take the first and last letters of the word on the left, followed by the first two letters of the word on the right.

5. 36/216

To find the number in the top line: starting with the first 1 in the upper square, and alternating upper and lower squares, square the numbers 1, 2, 3, 4, etc:

1 x 1=1, 2 x 2=4, 3 x 3=9, 4 x 4=16, 5 x 5= 25, 6 x 6=**36**, 7 x 7=49

To find the number in the lower line, repeat the process, cubing the numbers each time.

1 x 1 x 1=1, 2 x 2 x 2=8, 3 x 3 x 3=27, 4 x 4 x 4=64, 5 x 5 x 5=125, 6 x 6 x 6=**216**, 7 x 7 x 7=343

6. Picture 8

Each horizontal line shows the same three pictures in a different order.

7. 32

Starting with 1 and 2, each subsequent number is obtained by multiplying the two preceding ones:

1 x 2=2, 2 x 2=4, 2 x 4=8, 4 x 8=32

8. 1

On the first line, when arranged in the alphabet, the letters are each separated by four letters, on the second line, by three letters and on the third line by two letters.

9. Q

From C (the third letter of the alphabet), the sequence of the letters between the As corresponds to the sequence of prime numbers:

C (3)　E (5)　G (7)　K (11)　M (13)　Q (17)

10. Picture 4

The circle moves diagonally each time – first downwards and then upwards etc. In Picture 2, the circle is hidden by the left-hand square, which moves diagonally upwards. In Picture 3, they are both hidden by the right-hand square, which moves vertically upwards.

11. Picture 7

The picture on the right is made up on each line by adding together the top part of the first picture and the bottom part of the third picture.

12. Picture 6

The stripes on the right-hand side of each picture are alternately horizontal and vertical. The stripes on the left-hand side rotate by 45° each time.

13. EG/L

In the top row, the right-hand and left-hand letters form two sequences:

A	B	C	D	...	E
C	D	E	F	...	G

In the bottom row, each letter is separated by one, then two, then three, then four letters of the alphabet, working from the end of the alphabet.

Z (y) X (wv) U (tsr) Q (ponm) **L**

14. 8

In each circle, the number at the bottom is obtained by dividing the number on the left by the number on the right and multiplying the result by 2:

$$14 \div 7 = 2 \ (x \ 2) = \ 4$$
$$18 \div 3 = 6 \ (x \ 2) = 12$$
$$12 \div 3 = 4 \ (x \ 2) = \ 8$$

15. Sled

To form the word in brackets, take the last two letters of the word on the left, reversed, followed by the last two letters of the word on the right, also reversed.

16. Picture 5

On each line, first the outside circle and then the middle (second) circle change colour. The bull's eye remains the same throughout.

17. Picture 2

The square and the triangle turn clockwise 90° each time. The circle makes a quarter turn in the opposite direction.

18. 16

On each line, the last number is achieved by multiplying the first number by 4 and then by subtracting 4 from the obtained result:

$$3 \,(\times 4) = 12 \,(-4) = 8$$
$$7 \,(\times 4) = 28 \,(-4) = 24$$
$$5 \,(\times 4) = 20 \,(-4) = 16$$

19. P

The letters are arranged in a progression in alphabetical order:

B = first letter after A

D = second letter after B

G = third letter after D

K = fourth letter after G

P = fifth letter after K

20. Barge

SOLUTIONS: TEST 2

1. Picture 5

Each time, the circle and the triangle make a quarter turn clockwise and the square makes a quarter turn anticlockwise. Each shape changes colour with every move.

2. 5

The numbers correspond to the number of lines required to make up the Roman numerals that they follow.

3. Peel

The third and fifth letters of the first word are the first and third letters of the word in brackets. The third and fifth letters of the third word are the second and fourth letters of the word in brackets.

4. I

The position of each letter in the alphabet is given by the difference of the two numbers after the letter:

$$A = 1st\ (4-3)$$
$$C = 3rd\ (5-2)$$
$$E = 5th\ (6-1)$$
$$G = 7th\ (8-1)$$

5. 18

The number in brackets is obtained by adding together the individual figures that make up the numbers outside the brackets:

$$3 + 2 + 6 + 4 + 3 + 2 = 20$$
$$4 + 2 + 7 + 1 + 1 + 3 = 18$$

6. Picture 2

In each row, the picture on the right is obtained by superimposing the two preceding pictures. Any triangles outside the frame cancel each other out when they are superimposed.

7. Picture 2

The white square makes a quarter turn anticlockwise and changes colour with each move. The black circle makes a quarter turn clockwise and also changes colour. The black square makes a quarter turn clockwise with no colour change.

8. 2

In each row of numbers, the right-hand number is achieved by multiplying the two first numbers and then subtracting the third:

$$8 + 4 - 3 = 9$$
$$5 + 7 - 3 = 9$$
$$3 + 1 - 2 = 2$$

9. U

The letters are arranged in alphabetical order in an arithmetical progression, separated by one, then two, then three, then four and then five letters:

A (b) C (de) F (ghi) J (klmn) O (pqrst) U

10. Dear

To form the word in brackets, take the fourth letter of the word on the left, then the fourth letter of the word on the right, then the second letter of the word on the right and finally the first letter of the word on the left.

11. Picture 2

In each row, the third picture is obtained by changing the colour of the bull's eye in the first picture and the middle (second) circle of the second picture. The outer circle remains the same throughout.

12. P/E

The letters in the top row are separated in the alphabet by one letter, then two, then one, then two:

A (b) C (de) F (g) H (ij) K (l) M (no) **P**

The letters in the bottom row start at the end of the alphabet and increase the interval between the letters by one each time:

Z (–) Y (x) W (vu) T (srq) P (onml) K (jihgf) **E**

13. 4

The number in the middle of each triangle equals the product of both sides divided by the number at the bottom:

$3 \times 6 = 18 \div 9 = 2$

$6 \times 4 = 24 \div 8 = 3$

$8 \times 2 = 16 \div 4 = 4$

14. Draw

15. Picture 1

The square and the circles make a quarter turn clockwise. The black circle changes colour with each move.

16. Picture 3

In each row, the third picture is obtained by superimposing the preceding pictures. The triangles inside the frame move out, and those on the outside move in.

17. Picture 5

The circle moves horizontally in a 'zigzag' across the frame. The square moves along the diagonal.

18. 9/9

Start with the first number in the top row, and then, alternating between the rows, divide the numbers on the top row by 2 and multiply those on the bottom by 3:

$$4 (\div 2) = 2 (\times 3) = 6 (\div 2) = 3 (\times 3) = 9$$

Then, starting with the first number in the bottom row and again alternating between the rows multiply each number in the bottom row by 3 and divide by 2 those on the top row.

$$4 (\times 3) = 12 (\div 2) = 6 (\times 3) = 18 (\div 2) = 9$$

19. U

A, E, I, O, U is the order of the vowels in the alphabet.

20. Play

Replace each letter on the top line with the letter that precedes it in the alphabet.

TO EVALUATE YOUR IQ

Count up the questions you answered correctly – DON'T CHEAT!

Consult the graph below.

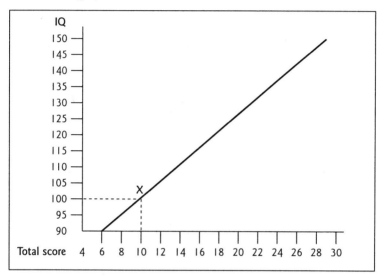

The graph above shows you how to convert your score to your IQ rating.

✳ First plot your total number of correct answers to both tests on the horizontal axis – in the example, the total number of correct answers is 10.

✳ Draw a perpendicular line up to the diagonal. This is point X.

✳ Draw a horizontal line from X to the vertical axis. The point where it meets the axis reveals your IQ value (in the example this is 100).

This evaluation is only valid if your score is in the range of 10 to 21 correct answers of the 40 questions (from both tests). It will not work if you score outside this range.

CHECK YOUR RATING

The following table shows your IQ rating compared to the population as a whole.

IQ	Intelligence level	Percentage of population
130 or more	Highly superior	2.2
120–129	Superior	6.7
110–119	Above average	16.1
90–109	Average	50.0
80–89	Below average	16.1
70–79	Inferior	6.7
69 or less	Inefficient	2.2

If you scored:

✳ 90–109: your IQ is average.

✳ 110–119: you are above average.

✳ 120–129: you are certainly in very good form at the moment and you have a strong aptitude for solving this sort of problem.

(For a more complete, in-depth evaluation of your performance, see *Measure Your IQ* by Gilles Azzopardi, also published by W. Foulsham and Co.)

If your score was lower than 90 (fewer than 10 correct answers) or higher than 130 (more than 21 correct answers), you cannot be categorised by this book. However, the likelihood of being either of these is slight. This type of test is not adapted to evaluate your IQ exactly.

CHAPTER 4

SHARPENING YOUR LOGIC

Reasoning is logical intelligence – which, generally speaking, is the ability to link judgements together to reach a conclusion.

Logic comes about in two ways: induction and deduction. Induction is the ability to reason from the particular to the general. For example, in a test, it is all about understanding the relationship between two elements so that you can apply this to a third element. Deduction is the mental process that enables you to conclude something from given premises. This is the ability to reason from the general to the particular.

The following exercises are designed to develop both types of logic, but they also enable you to evaluate precisely your level of logical intelligence.

They are presented in two series of 20 problems, each to be solved in 15 minutes. That's just under one minute per question, so don't waste time trying to solve a problem that you're stuck on. Move on to the next.

However, you don't have to do both tests immediately one after the other. You can take time out in between. It doesn't even matter if you do one test one day and the other the next. The important thing is that you wait until you've finished both tests to evaluate your results.

SERIES A

NB: You have 15 minutes to solve 20 problems.

Test 1: Underline the next number in the series or insert the correct numbers where appropriate:

1.   7 1 3 4 2 6 3 8 7 4 7 9 5 1
2.   1 5 9 13 ?
3.   5 2 4 1 3 ?
4.   3 6 5 10 9 ?
5.   0 2 6 12 ?
6.   3 6 5 15 14 ? ?
7.   5 3 1 6 7 3 4 6 8 9 5 7 1
8.   3 9 27 81 ? ?
9.   7 13 8 12 ? 11 ?
10.   1 4 9 16 27 40 ?

Test 2: Insert the correct letters in the gaps:

1.   DBAC HFEG LJIK PNM-
2.   A D I P -
3.   A Z BC YX DEF - - -
4.   A D G J -
5.   AE BF CG DH -
6.   A C E G I - -
7.   C G L R -
8.   F I M P -
9.   M P K R I T -
10.   E J - Z

SERIES B

NB: You have 15 minutes to solve 20 problems.

Test 3: Insert the appropriate letters or words in the gaps.

1.	12 B	23 F	34 L	45 -		
2.	J	2	G	5	D	8	-	-
3.	211	911	I	11;	T	N	O	-
4.	A1	BC2	DEF6	GHIJ - -		
5.	12	A1	R3	AIR		
	M3	O2	A4	N5	W1	- - - - -
6.	36	(face)	15			
	48	(- - - -)	51			
7.	N3	12	G1	A4	GINA	
	L5 I7 R3 N8 G1 E9 D6 E2 A4 - - - - - - - -					
8.	TRAINS 132654 RAT 432					
	STAIN 63487 RAIN - - -					

Test 4: Sequences of pictures

1. Find the picture to complete the sequence:

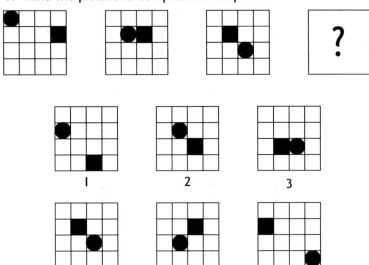

2. Find the picture to complete the sequence:

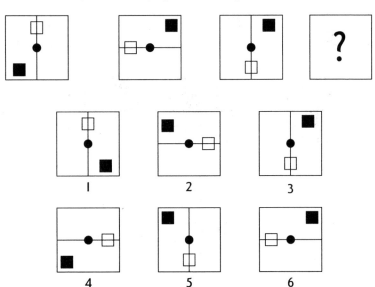

3. Find the picture to complete the sequence:

1   2   3

4   5   6

4. Find the picture to complete the sequence:

1   2   3

4   5   6

5. Find the picture to complete the sequence

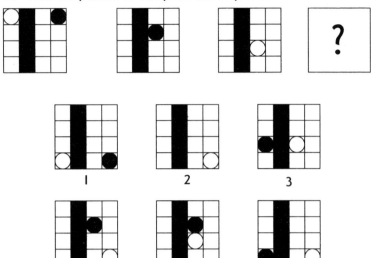

6. Find the picture to complete the sequence:

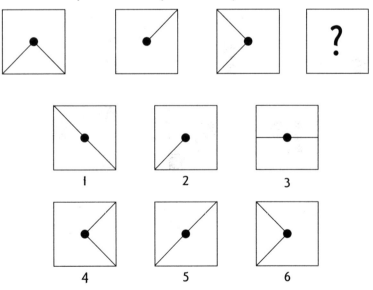

7. Find the picture to complete the sequence:

1   2   3

  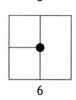

4   5   6

8. Find the picture to complete the sequence:

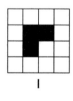

1   2   3

4   5   6

9. Find the picture to complete the sequence:

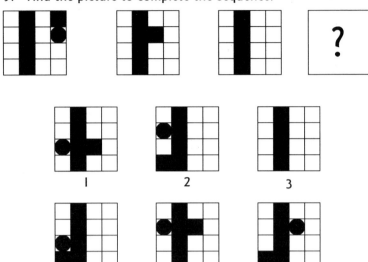

10. Find the picture to complete the sequence:

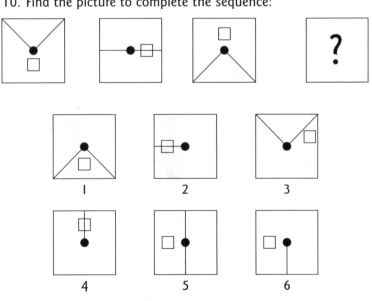

11. Find the picture to complete the sequence:

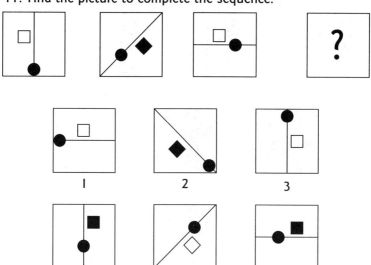

12. Find the picture to complete the sequence:

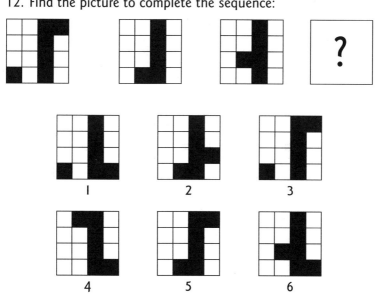

SOLUTIONS: SERIES A

Test 1: Sequences of numbers

1.   7 <u>1</u> 3 4 <u>2</u> 6 <u>3</u> 8 7 <u>4</u> 7 9 <u>5</u> 1

The series is 1,2,3,4,5.

2.   1   5   9   13   17

Add 4 to each number to obtain the next in the series.

3.   5   2   4   1   3   0

The series is obtained by alternately adding 3 and subtracting 2:
5 (– 3) = 2 (+2) = 4 (–3) = 1 (+2) = 3 (–3) = **0**

4.   3   6   5   10   9   18

The series is obtained by alternately multiplying by 2 and subtracting 1:

3 (×2) = 6 (–1) = 5 (×2) = 10 (–1) = 9 (×2) = **18**

5.   0   2   6   12   **20**

The series is obtained by taking the sequence 1,2,3,4,5 and then squaring each figure and subtracting its own value from the result:
$1^2 – 1 = 0, 2^2 – 2 = 2, 3^2 – 3 = 6, 4^2 – 4 = 12, 5^2 – 5 = $ **20**

6.   3   6   5   15   14   56   **55**

Multiply the first figure by 2, then subtract 1. Multiply this figure by 3 and subtract 1. Multiply by 4 and subtract 1, etc.
3 (×2) = 6 (–1) = 5 (×3) = 15 (–1) = 14 (×4) = **56** (–1) = **55**

7.   5 3 <u>1</u> 6 7 3 <u>4</u> 6 8 <u>9</u> 5 7 1

The series is the sequence of numbers, starting at 1, squared.

8.   3   9   27   81   **243**   **729**

Each number is obtained by multiplying the one before by 3.

9.   7 13 8 12 9 11 10

Add 6 to the first number, subtract 5 from the next, add 4 to the next, subtract 3 etc:
7 (+6) = 13 (–5) = 8 (+4) = 12 (–3) = 9 (+2) = 11 (–1) = 10

10.   1 4 9 16 27 40 57

Start by adding 3 to the first number. Thereafter, add the prime numbers in sequence to each number:
1 (+3) = 4 (+5) = 9 (+7) = 16 (+11) = 27 (+13) = 40 + 17 = 57

Test 2: Sequences of letters

1.   DBAC HFEG LJIK PNMO

In each group, the last letter is the one that precedes the first in the alphabet.

2.   A D I P Y

The position of each letter in the alphabet, taken as a number, corresponds to the squares of the sequence of numbers 1,2,3,4,5.

3.   A Z BC YX DEF WVU

There are two alphabetical series of letters here, one starting at the beginning of the alphabet and one at the end. Both increase by one letter each time. A BC DEF and Z YX WVU.

4.   A D G J M

Each letter is separated by two others in the alphabet:
A (bc) D (ef) G (hi) J (kl) M

5.   AE BF CG DH EI

The letters on the left and right of each pair form two series in alphabetical order: A,B,C,D,E and E,F,G,H,I.

6. A C E G I **K** M

There are two separate sequences of letters, separated by three other letters in the alphabet: A (bcd) E (fgh) I (jkl) **M**, and C (def) G (hij) **K**

7. C G L R

Each letter is situated centrally in the letters of the alphabet grouped between two vowels:
b C d (e) f G h (i) j k L m n (o) p q R s t (u)

8. F I M P T

Each letter is separated from the one that follows it in the alphabet by two and three letters alternately: F (gh) I (jkl) M (no) P (qrs) T

9. M P K R I T G

In this series, the number of letters separating each letter in the alphabet is the progression 2, 4, 6, 8, 10, 12, with the order reversing each time: M (no) P (onml) K (lmnopq) R (qponmlkj) I (jklmnopqrs) T (srqponmlkjih) G

10. E J Q Z

Taking the positions of the letters in the alphabet as numbers (5, 10, 17 and 26), these are the squares of the sequence of numbers 2, 3, 4, 5, plus 1.

SOLUTIONS: SERIES B

Test 3: Sequences of letters and numbers

1. 12B 23F 34L 45T

The product of the numbers gives the position of the letter in the alphabet: 4 x 5 = 20 = T, the twentieth letter.

2.   J 2 G 5 D 8 A 11

Each letter is separated from the one following by two letters in the alphabet, in reverse order. Each number is obtained by adding 3 to the one before.

3.   211 911 1 11; T N O E

The letters are the initials of the numbers when written in full: Ten; Nine hundred and eleven; One; Eleven

4.   A1 BC2 DEF6 GHIJ24

Each number is obtained by multiplying the one before by the number of letters that follow it.

5.   12   A1   R3   AIR

       M3   O2   A4   N5   W1   **WOMAN**

The numbers indicate the positions of the letters to make up the words 'air' and 'woman'.

6.   Head

In each case, the two pairs of numbers give the positions in the alphabet of the letters of the words in brackets, which are then rearranged to give the word.

7.   N3 12 G1 A4 GINA

       L5 17 R3 N8 G1 E9 D6 E2 A4 **GERALDINE**

The numbers give the order of the letters in a name.

8.   TRAINS   132654   RAT 432

       STAIN   63487   RAIN **6598**

The sequence of numbers next to TRAINS is a code with each letter corresponding to a number. The other words are formed with the letters of TRAINS and their numbers but, in the first instance (for RAT) the numbers are increased by 1, for STAIN they are increased by 2 and for RAIN they are increased by 3.

Test 4: Sequences of pictures

1. Picture 6

The circle descends diagonally from left to right. The square moves horizontally from right to left.

2. Picture 4

The line and the white square rotate through 90° anticlockwise each time. The black square moves in the same way but it alternates from the left to the right of the line.

3. Picture 3

The line and the circles rotate each time by 45° clockwise. The circles (or any part of them) are black when they are in the bottom half of the square and white when in the top half of the square.

4. Picture 3

The circle moves horizontally from right to left and the square moves diagonally from the bottom to the top of the grid.

5. Picture 6

The white circle and the black circle move diagonally from the top to the bottom of the grid.

6. Picture 5

The line on the left rotates clockwise each time through 180°. The line on the right moves through 90° anticlockwise.

7. Picture 1

The horizontal line remains static. The other two lines rotate through 45° anticlockwise.

8. Picture 4

The three squares each move one box vertically, diagonally and horizontally respectively.

9. Picture 2

The square moves by one box diagonally and the circle moves by one box horizontally from right to left.

10. Picture 6

The line on the right rotates each time through 45° clockwise. The line on the left rotates through 45° anticlockwise. The square makes a quarter turn anticlockwise.

11. Picture 2

The central line rotates each time through 45° clockwise. The black circle progresses a quarter of the way further along the line. The square moves from one side to the other of the line and changes colour.

12. Picture 1

The square at the top moves diagonally downwards by one box. The square at the bottom moves horizontally from left to right.

EVALUATING YOUR RESULTS

Fill in your scores in the table below so you can see them altogether.

SERIES A	SERIES B
Test 1: Sequence of numbers	Test 3: Sequences of letters and numbers
(10 problems) Total correct answers:	(8 problems) Total correct answers:
Test 2:Sequence of letters	Test 4: Sequences of pictures
(10 problems) Total correct answers:	(12 problems) Total correct answers:

Total number of problems: 40

Total number of correct answers:

You can evaluate your results in several ways: overall, by looking at your score in each test, or by comparing your scores in different kinds of test.

Overall

Your results are valid if your score total is in the range of 6 to 22 correct answers. If you scored above or below this number you are not made for this test or the test is not made for you.

✳ 6–14 correct answers

Average. You show a lack of precision if you scored nearer 6. You show an aptitude for abstract thought if you scored nearer 14.

✳ 15–18 correct answers

You are very logical, you have excellent judgment and powers of analysis. You reason clearly although you may sometimes be a little too rigid.

✳ 18–22 correct answers

You have impeccable logic and are capable of an astonishing degree of abstract thought. Too much, really. You could probably do with a little emotional intelligence to round off your attitudes.

Test by test

✳ If you scored less than 3 points in Tests 1, 2 or 3, or less than 4 points in Test 4, you have a weakness in the area tested.

✳ On the other hand, you show strength if you scored 4 points or more in Tests 1, 2 or 3, or 5 points or more in Test 4.

By comparison

✳ Compare your results for Tests 1 and 2: You have greater aptitude for deduction if you have a better score in the number tests. You have greater powers of inductive thinking if you scored better in the letters tests.

✳ Compare your results for Tests 3 and 4: You have a more 'conceptual' form of intelligence if you scored better in the number and letters sequences. Your intelligence is more 'visual' if you were more successful in the picture sequences.

CHAPTER 5

STIMULATING YOUR MEMORY

The memory is a very complex function of your brain. It can carry out four distinctly different operations on any one given piece of information. These can be defined as follows:

✳ **Capture:** registering a piece of information in your mind

✳ **Conservation:** storing the information

✳ **Recall:** recollecting the information when required

✳ **Recognition:** the identification and locating of stored information

Each of these operations can be relatively autonomous. For example, the calling up of a stored piece of information by the memory corresponds to a voluntary recollection. On the other hand, a vague memory of something is due to an involuntary recollection.

Identification is the ability to recognise something as a record of the past, and to recall a memory. Locating it consists of being able to restore this memory in its temporal context.

You can also distinguish a type of immediate memory where there is no back-up of information, no mnemonic fixing it in your mind. This is what happens when you learn something by heart. This type of memory is different from a memory of the past, or recorded memory.

The following exercises are designed to activate all the different functions of the memory. They allow you to stimulate your mnemonic capacities, and also to evaluate the actual capacity of your memory.

EXERCISING YOUR IMMEDIATE MEMORY

This test comprises four sequences of numbers. Read each line once and then store it in your memory. You can take a break between sequences. Check your performance after sequences 1 and 2. Sequences 3 and 4 will show how efficient you are at picking something up.

Note: This test is usually carried out by a tester who reads out each sequence at a rate of one number per second. The subject then repeats the sequence. When a mistake is made, the tester reads out a revised sequence which includes the same number of figures. If the subject can repeat this sequence, the tester moves on to the next. If not, this test is finished. After a break, the tester moves on to the second test, in which the subject must repeat each sequence of figures starting with the last figure read out.

If you get someone else to test you in this way, your scores will be even more accurate. However, you can do the test by yourself.

Sequence I

Carefully read each line of numbers once and rewrite it from memory.

4	7	I						
2	5	8	4					
I	3	6	2	8				
5	4	I	3	7	9			
2	5	7	3	6	3	7		
3	I	6	2	5	8	7	2	
9	5	7	7	5	3	8	I	6

Sequence 2

Carefully read each line of numbers once and rewrite it from memory in reverse order.

4	6	I						
2	4	I	7					
3	2	4	I	2				
5	8	7	3	5	2			
9	5	4	7	8	3	I		
I	3	7	9	6	4	4	I	
3	7	5	3	9	8	5	3	2

Checking your scores

Note down the greatest number of figures that you have been able to recall in the correct order, both forwards and backwards.

Sequence 3

Carefully read each line of numbers once and rewrite it from memory.

3	6	2						
7	4	6	1					
1	3	7	9	5				
6	8	5	7	1	9			
1	5	1	2	7	7	4		
6	3	9	6	4	1	4	3	
5	7	9	8	2	9	1	7	3

Sequence 4

Carefully read each line of numbers once and rewrite it from memory in reverse order.

Checking your scores

Note down the greatest number of figures that you have been able to recall in the correct order – both forwards and backwards. Compare these scores to the previous ones and keep only your best score.

EVALUATING YOUR IMMEDIATE MEMORY

* An adult of 'average' intelligence should be able to repeat five figures in the order they are given and three in reverse order.

* You are above average if you have been able to recall between six and eight forwards and four to six backwards.

* You have an excellent memory if you can get nine correct forwards and between seven and nine backwards.

EXERCISING YOUR RECORDED MEMORY

The following test is designed to stimulate and evaluate your overall memory and each of its specific functions: capture, conservation, recollection and recognition.

The test comprises a series of seven exercises all based on one set of pictures. You will need a pencil, a rubber and a piece of paper for this test.

sun

house

tree

car

cat

plane

flower

table

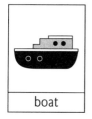

boat

bird

television

glasses

bicycle

lamp

fish

apple

chair

book

scissors

carrot

Exercise 1

Here is the set of pictures. From memory, write under each one the
word that corresponds to it.

Exercise 2

Here are the same pictures, but represented by stylised symbols. From memory, write under each one the word that corresponds to it.

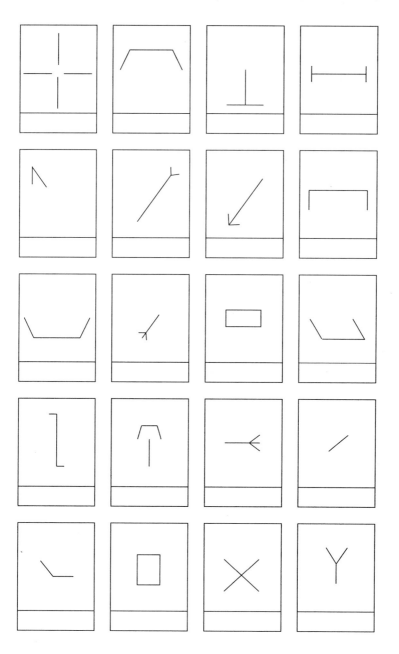

Exercise 3

Here are the same symbols once more but in a different order. From memory, write the corresponding word under each one.

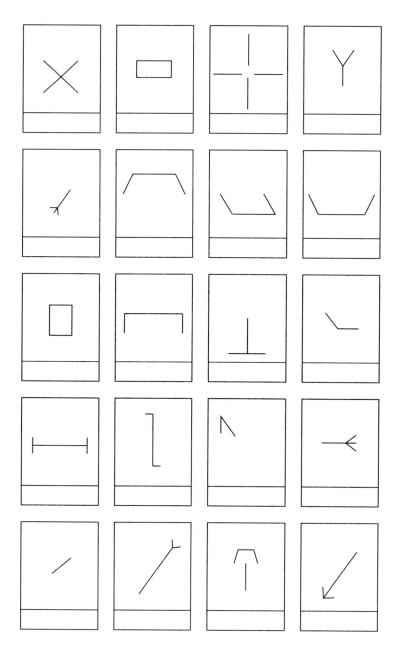

Exercise 4

Here is the original set of pictures. From memory, write the corresponding words under each picture.

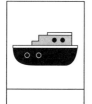

Exercise 5

Here is the original picture grid, empty. Fill in the pictures and their corresponding words. The order is not important.

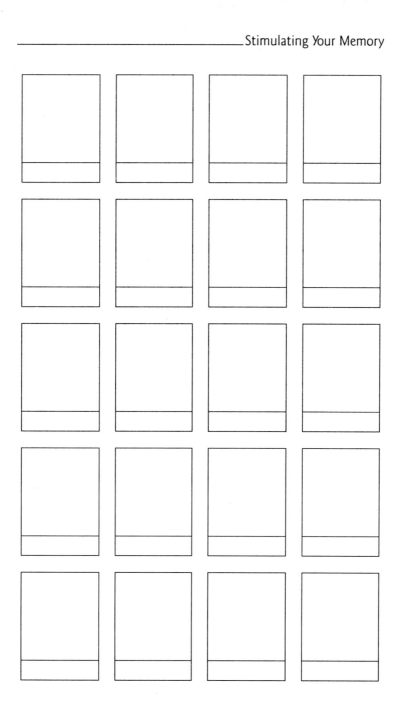

Exercise 6

Now turn to another chapter or close the book and do something else to occupy yourself for 20 minutes. Then, without looking back at this chapter, write down as many of the words corresponding to the pictures that you can recall from memory in exactly 20 minutes. Use a stopwatch or timer to time yourself.

_____ _____ _____ _____

_____ _____ _____ _____

_____ _____ _____ _____

_____ _____ _____ _____

_____ _____ _____ _____

Exercise 7

Here is a list of 40 words. Underline the 20 words that correspond to the set of pictures you memorised.

crab	sun	armchair	house	box
tie	crayon	car	tree	cat
book	scissors	shell	pear	horse
pear	aeroplane	flower	ashtray	radio
boat	bird	cigar	table	umbrella
egg	glasses	knife	chimney	television
carrot	bicycle	lamp	key	telephone
apple	fish	chair	trombone	shoe

TO EVALUATE YOUR MEMORY

Check your results and note in the boxes how many correct answers for each exercise you scored out of 20.

Exercise 1
This stimulates your memory and allows you to evaluate your ability to recall information. Average score: 8–9 out of 20.

Exercise 2
This stimulates and evaluates your functions of recognition and spatial memory. Average score: 7–8 out of 20.

Exercise 3
This stimulates the ability of your primitive memory to function independently from your spatial memory. Average score: 6–7 out of 20.

Exercise 4
This exercise stimulates your abilities to store and recall information. Average score: 8–9 out of 20.

Exercise 5
This exercise stimulates your powers of recollection, evaluating your voluntary memory. Average score: 8–9 out of 20.

Exercise 6
This evaluates and stimulates your powers of conservation and recollection. Average score: 8–9 out of 20.

Exercise 7
This is to evaluate your powers of recognition and identification. You should achieve close to 20 out of 20.

CHAPTER 6

IMPROVING YOUR UNDERSTANDING

Man is a talking being, and there is no intelligence without language. Verbal intelligence refers to an essential ability: comprehension. This ability plays a principal role in academic, social and professional success, and occupies a special place amongst the other forms of intelligence. In fact, without comprehension the other forms of intelligence can not be understood, expressed or used.

The following 60 problems are designed to stimulate your powers of comprehension.

60 COMPREHENSION PROBLEMS

1. Mind is to thought what body is to:

     flesh   idea   action   letter   soul

2. The opposite of rudimentary is:

   elementary   developed   refined   complementary   sophisticated

3. Which is the odd one out?

     pontoon   bridge   lady   poker   blackjack

4. The synonym of homogeneous is:

    mixed   equivocal   uniform   symmetrical   heterogeneous

5. A corollary is:

     a   the corona around the sun

     b   a coronary artery

     c   a direct consequence

     d   a group of petals

6. Find the word, a synonym of group, that makes two others when combined with the letters outside the brackets:

     bas ... (- - -) ... ter

7. Insert in the brackets a word that has the same meaning as the other two words.

     champagne (- - - - - -) effervescent

8. Volume is to cube as surface area is to:

     depth   pressure   square   width

9. The opposite of emit is:

    remit   receive   omit   demean   replace

10. Which is the odd one out?

    guitar   harp   mandolin   double bass   saxophone   violin

11. Imminent is a synonym of:

    fatal   inescapable   inevitable   near   necessary   famous

12. Anorexia is:

    a   an exception to the rules

    b   gradually losing one's sense of smell

    c   having no sense of smell

    d   loss of appetite

13. Find a word that makes two others with the letters outside the brackets

    be ... (- - - -) ... car

14. Insert in the brackets a word that has the same meaning as the other two words:

    score (- - - -) label

15. The microscope is to the infinitely small what the telescope is to the infinitely:

    big   far   high   near   fast   close

16. The opposite of sectarian is:

    secular   partisan   public   liberal   regular   nomadic

17. Which is the odd one out?

    border   pasture   square   prairie   flowerbed   meadow

18. The synonym of conspicuous is:

    arrogant   uncertain   solid   precise   apparent   authentic

19. A stereotype is:

    a   a recording

    b   a preformed impression

    c   a prototype video

    d   an abridged version

20. Insert a word that makes two others when combined with the other two words:

egg (---) cake

21. Insert in the brackets a word that has the same meaning as the other two words:

load (-----) responsibility

22. Week is to month as hour is to:

minute   second   day   evening

23. The opposite of innate is:

instinctive natural hereditary acquired atavistic native

24. Which is the odd one out?

turbot   john dory   dab   sole   whiting   skate

25. The synonym of inexplicable is:

unaccountable ineffable priceless incomprehensible unspeakable

26. A mediator is:

    a   a media professional

    b   a medial planner

    c   a conciliator

    d   a media personality

27. Find a word that makes two others when added to the letters outside the brackets

    ear ... (- - - -) ... let

28. Insert in the brackets a word that has the same meaning as the other two words:

    profit (- - - - - - - -) attention

29. Cow is to calf as hen is to:

    chick   chicken   capon   pullet   cockerel

30. The opposite of shaded is:

    coloured   iridescent   illuminated   variegated   shimmering

31. Which is the odd one out?

    parachute   parabola   partition   parasol   parados

32. What is the synonym of verification?

    establishment   revision   restoration   reconstruction
    reparation

33. A seminar is:

    a   a sac of spermatozoa

    b   a weekly review

    c   a work meeting

    d   a bracelet with seven links

34. Find the word, a synonym of loaned, that forms two others when added to the letters outside the brackets:

    ta ...   (- - - -)   ... il

35. Insert in the brackets a word that means the same as the other two words:

    pond (- - - -) supply

36. Sour is to sugary as dry is to:

   cold   bitter   humid   sweet   hard   hot

37. The opposite of hardly is:

   rarely   much   little   briefly   never   often

38. Which is the odd one out?

   shrimp   crayfish   lobster   Dublin Bay prawn

39. The synonym of orthodox is:

   suitable   contrary   contradictory   true   questionable

40. A collation is:

   a   a member of one's family

   b   a light meal

   c   a collage

   d   a cardiac arrest

41. Find a word that forms two others when added to the letters outside the brackets

   fore ... (- - -) ... age

42. Insert in the brackets a word that has the same meaning as the other two words:

   arm (- - - - - -) adherent

43. Ivory is to elephant as cashmere is to:

   Himalayas   rabbit   goat   pullover

44. The opposite of voluble is:

   vague   muffled   silent   talkative   slow-moving

45. Which is the odd one out?

   hemp   cotton   jute   raffia   linen   silk

46. The synonym of extravagant is:

astonishing magnificent surprising generous considerable

47. A pundit is:

     a   a religious leader

     b   a cliche

     c   an ovation

     d   an expert

48. Find a word that makes two others when added to the letters outside the brackets

moon ... (-----) ... house

49. Insert in the brackets a word that has the same meaning as the other two words:

resort (------) focus

50. Word is to phrase as letter is to:

spirit word writer name alphabet figure

51. The opposite of monologue is:

analogue homologue epilogue dialogue prologue

52. Which is the odd one out?

stone type finger down line paper

53. The synonym of ethical is:

traditional moral native religious essential

54. A sinecure is:

      a a Chinese room

      b a treatment for sinusitis

      c a no-effort situation

      d a thermal spa for cinema fans

55. Find a word that forms two others with the letters outside the brackets

pi ... (----) ... able

56. Insert in the brackets one word that has the same meaning as the other two words

finch (-------) decoration

57. London is to gin what Bombay is to:

cinema   fish   brandy   duck   bosom

58. The opposite of specious is:

spacious   serious   special   spatial   spiral   classified

59. Which is the odd one out?

sticky   viscous   nauseous   viscid   glutinous

60. The synonym of regress is:

remove   deplore   repulse   bear down   move back
dwindle

SOLUTIONS

1. Action

2. Developed

3. Lady. The others are the names of card games.

4. Uniform

5. A direct consequence

6. Set. This forms the words basset and setter.

7. Bubbly

8. Square

9. Receive

10. Saxophone. The others are stringed instruments.

11. Near

12. Loss of appetite

13. Side. This forms the words beside and sidecar.

14. Mark

15. Far

16. Liberal

17. Square. The others are all pieces of cultivated land.

18. Apparent

19. A preformed impression

20. Cup

21. Burden

22. Day

23. Acquired

24. Skate. You eat the wings, not the flesh.

25. Unaccountable

26. A conciliator

27. Ring. This forms the words earring and ringlet.

28. Interest

29. Chick

30. Illuminated

31. Parabola (a symmetrical curve). The others are all means of protection.

32. Establishment

33. A work meeting

34. Lent. This gives the words talent and lentil.

35. Pool

36. Humid

37. Much

38. Crayfish is the only crustacean that is found in fresh water.

39. True

40. A light meal

41. Man. This forms the words foreman and manage.

42. Member

43. Goat

44. Silent

45. Silk. The others are vegetable fibres.

46. Generous

47. Expert

48. Light. This forms the words moonlight and lighthouse.

49. Centre

50. Word

51. Dialogue

52. Finger. All the others form new words when prefixed with the word touch.

53. Moral

54. A no-effort situation

55. Rate. This forms the words pirate and rateable.

56. Bunting

57. Duck

58. Serious

59. Nauseous. All the others mean gluey.

60. Move back

YOUR SCORE

Score one point for every correct answer. Add up the total number of points you scored and divide by 2 to give you your average score. This will be a number between 0 and 30.

❋ Less than 12 points

Your powers of comprehension are somewhat lacking and your vocabulary is rather limited. You need to develop a wider, less subjective, understanding of the meaning of words.

❋ 13–22 points

You are average, or slightly above average if you scored more than 17 points. You are quite knowledgeable, but your intelligence is more concrete than conceptual. You don't always use words correctly.

❋ More than 22 points

You have excellent powers of comprehension and a high level of general knowledge.

CHAPTER 7

ENRICHING YOUR VOCABULARY

Word usage, or the verbal factor, has an effect on our comprehension and the ability to make ourselves understood.

Word knowledge, or what we may call the lexical factor, is essential to intelligence in as much as it is intimately linked to speech. It concerns our ability to produce words rapidly within given constraints such as the number and position of letters, or the inclusion of prefixes and rhyme.

The following 40 problems are designed to help you increase your abilities in this field.

VOCABULARY PROBLEMS

Give yourself 30 minutes to solve them (this is less than 1 minute per problem).

1. Write down 12 words starting and finishing with a:

   1 a......a 2 a......a 3 a......a 4 a......a

   5 a......a 6 a......a 7 a......a 8 a......a

   9 a......a 10 a......a 11 a......a 12 a......a

2. Write down 12 three-letter words:

   1 .... 2 .... 3 .... 4 ....

   5 .... 6 .... 7 .... 8 ....

   9 .... 10 .... 11 .... 12 ....

3. Write down eight words starting with aba:

   1 aba..... 2 aba..... 3 aba..... 4 aba.....

   5 aba..... 6 aba..... 7 aba..... 8 aba.....

4. Write down 12 words finishing with -ous:

   1 ......ous 2 ......ous 3 ......ous 4 ......ous

   5 ......ous 6 ......ous 7 ......ous 8 ......ous

   9 ......ous 10 ......ous 11 ......ous 12 .....ous

5. Find a three-letter word that forms another word when added to each of these letters:

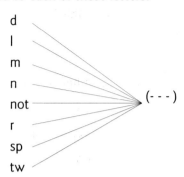

d
l
m
n
not
r
sp
tw

(- - -)

6. Write down 12 words that start with i and finish with –on:

1 i.....on	2 i.....on	3 i.....on	4 i.....on
5 i.....on	6 i.....on	7 i.....on	8 i.....on
9 i.....on	10 i.....on	11 i.....on	12 i.....on

7. Write down 12 four-letter words:

1	2	3	4 ....
5	6	7	8 ....
9	10	11	12 ....

8. Write down 12 words that start with pro:

1 pro.....	2 pro.....	3 pro.....	4 pro.....
5 pro.....	6 pro.....	7 pro.....	8 pro.....
9 pro.....	10 pro.....	11 pro.....	12 pro.....

9. Write down 12 words finishing with –ard:

1 .....ard	2 .....ard	3 .....ard	4 .....ard
5 .....ard	6 .....ard	7 .....ard	8 .....ard
9 .....ard	10 .....ard	11 .....ard	12 .....ard

10. Find a three-letter word that forms another word when added to each of these letters:

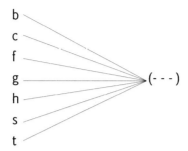

```
b
c
f
g ────────────► (- - -)
h
s
t
```

11. Write down 12 words starting and finishing with e:

1 e . . . . . e	2 e . . . . . e	3 e . . . . . e	4 e . . . . . e
5 e . . . . . e	6 e . . . . . e	7 e . . . . . e	8 e . . . . . e
9 e . . . . . e	10 e . . . . . e	11 e . . . . . e	12 e . . . . . e

12. Write down 12 five-letter words:

1	2	3	4 . . . .
5	6	7	8 . . . .
9	10	11	12 . . . .

13. Write down 12 words starting with im:

1 im	2 im	3 im	4 im . . . . .
5 im	6 im	7 im	8 im . . . . .
9 im	10 im	11 im	12 im . . . . .

14. Write down eight words ending with -gram:

| 1 . . . . . gram | 2 . . . . . gram | 3 . . . . . gram | 4 . . . . . gram |
| 5 . . . . . gram | 6 . . . . . gram | 7 . . . . . gram | 8 . . . . . gram |

15. Find a four-letter word that forms another word when added to each of these letters:

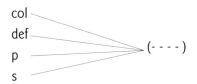

16. Write down 12 words starting and finishing with t:

    I t . . . . . t   2 t . . . . . t   3 t . . . . . t   4 t . . . . . t

    5 t . . . . . t   6 t . . . . . t   7 t . . . . . t   8 t . . . . . t

    9 t . . . . . t   10 t . . . . . t   II t . . . . . t   12 t . . . . . t

17. Write down 12 six-letter words:

    I . . . .   2 . . . .   3 . . . .   4 . . . .

    5 . . . .   6 . . . .   7 . . . .   8 . . . .

    9 . . . .   10 . . . .   II . . . .   12 . . . .

18. Write down 12 words beginning with trans:

    I trans . . .   2 trans . . .   3 trans . . .   4 trans . . .

    5 trans . . .   6 trans . . .   7 trans . . .   8 trans . . .

    9 trans . . .   10 trans . . .   II trans . . .   12 trans . . .

19. Write down 12 words finishing with –ail:

    I . . . . . ail   2 . . . . . ail   3 . . . . . ail   4 . . . . . ail

    5 . . . . . ail   6 . . . . . ail   7 . . . . . ail   8 . . . . . ail

    9 . . . . . ail   10 . . . . . ail   II . . . . . ail   12 . . . . . ail

20. Find a four-letter word that forms another word when prefixed by each of these letters:

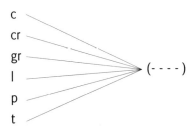

c

cr

gr

l

p

t

(- - - -)

21. Write down five words starting and ending with w:

    1 w . . . . . w   2 w . . . . . w   3 w . . . . . w

    4 w . . . . . w   5 w . . . . . w

22. Write down 12 seven-letter words:

    1 . . . .   2 . . . .   3 . . . .   4 . . . .

    5 . . . .   6 . . . .   7 . . . .   8 . . . .

    9 . . . .   10 . . . .   11 . . . .   12 . . . .

23. Write down 12 words starting with com:

    1 com . . .   2 com . . .   3 com . . .   4 com . . .

    5 com . . .   6 com . . .   7 com . . .   8 com . . .

    9 com . . .   10 com . . .   11 com . . .   12 com . . .

24. Write down 12 words finishing with –able:

    1 . . . . . able   2 . . . . . able   3 . . . . . able   4 . . . . . able

    5 . . . . . able   6 . . . . . able   7 . . . . . able   8 . . . . . able

    9 . . . . . able   10 . . . . able   11 . . . . able   12 . . . . able

25. Find a three-letter word that forms another other word when prefixed by each of these letters:

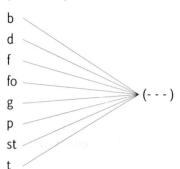

b
d
f
fo
g
p
st
t

(- - -)

26. Write down 12 words starting and finishing with l:

  1 l l   2 l l   3 l l   4 l l

  5 l l   6 l l   7 l l   8 l l

  9 l l   10l l   11l .....l 12l l

27. Write down 12 eight-letter words:

  1 ....   2 ....   3 ....   4 ....

  5 ....   6 ....   7 ....   8 ....

  9 ....   10 ....   11 .... 12 ....

28. Write down 12 words starting with pre:

  1 pre ....   2 pre ....   3 pre ....   4 pre ....

  5 pre ....   6 pre ....   7 pre ....   8 pre ....

  9 pre ....   10 pre ....   11 pre .... 12 pre ....

29. Write down 12 words ending with –et:

  1 ......et   2 ......et   3 ......et   4 ......et

  5 ......et   6 ......et   7 ......et   8 ......et

  9 ......et   10 .....et   11 .....et   12 .....et

30. Find a three-letter word that forms another word when prefixed by each of these letters:

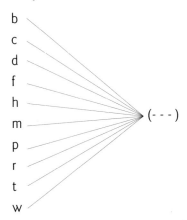

b
c
d
f
h
m
p
r
t
w

(- - -)

31. Write down 12 words starting and finishing with n:

1 n.....n	2 n.....n	3 n.....n	4 n.....n
5 n.....n	6 n.....n	7 n.....n	8 n.....n
9 n.....n	10 n.....n	11 n.....n	12 n.....n

32. Write down 12 nine-letter words:

1	2	3	4 ....
5	6	7	8 ....
9	10	11	12 ....

33. Write down 12 words starting with bi:

1 bi.....	2 bi.....	3 bi.....	4 bi.....
5 bi.....	6 bi.....	7 bi.....	8 bi.....
9 bi.....	10 bi.....	11 bi.....	12 bi.....

34. Write down 8 words ending with –ogue:

| 1 ....ogue | 2 ....ogue | 3 ....ogue | 4 ....ogue |
| 5 ....ogue | 6 ....ogue | 7 ....ogue | 8 ....ogue |

35. Find a three-letter word that forms another word when prefixed by each of these letters:

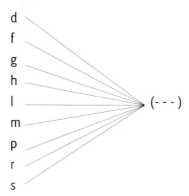

d
f
g
h
l   (- - -)
m
p
r
s

36. Find 12 words that start and end with r:

   I r . . . . . r   2 r . . . . . r   3 r . . . . . r   4 r . . . . . r

   5 r . . . . . r   6 r . . . . . r   7 r . . . . . r   8 r . . . . . r

   9 r . . . . . r   10 r . . . . . r   II r . . . . . r   12 r . . . . . r

37. Write down 12 ten-letter words:

   I   2   3   4   . . . .

   5   6   7   8   . . . .

   9   . . . .   10 . . . .   II . . . .   12 . . . .

38. Write down 12 words starting with sub:

   I sub . . . .   2 sub . . . .   3 sub . . . .   4 sub . . . .

   5 sub . . . .   6 sub . . . .   7 sub . . . .   8 sub . . . .

   9 sub . . . .   10 sub . . . .   II sub . . . .   12 sub . . . .

39. Write down 12 words ending with –ance:

    I . . . . ance   2 . . . . ance   3 . . . . ance   4 . . . . ance

    5 . . . . ance   6 . . . . ance   7 . . . . ance   8 . . . . ance

    9 . . . . ance 10 . . . . ance 11 . . . . ance 12 . . . . ance

40. Find a three-letter word that forms another word when prefixed by each of these letters:

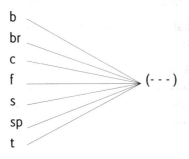

```
b
br
c
f        (- - -)
s
sp
t
```

SOLUTIONS

1. Arena, antenna, area, aria, alpha, alfalfa, alleluia, angora, analgesia, anathema, angina, anima, anorexia, aorta, apnoea, apologia, asthma, azalea, abracadabra, abscissa, alpaca, amnesia, ammonia, amoeba, ambrosia, amphora, anaemia, etc.

2. There are literally thousands of three-letter words.

3. Aback, abacus, abaft, abalone, abandon, abase, abash, abate, abattoir, abaya, etc.

4. There are dozens of words ending with –ous: humorous, vivacious, mendacious, pugnacious, tremendous, fractious, adventurous, advantageous, mountainous, glorious, envious, poisonous, curious, obsequious, monstrous, homogeneous, nauseous, viscous, nutritious, etc.

5. Ice, giving dice, lice, mice, nice, notice, rice, spice and twice.

6. Iron, icon, irritation, irrigation, iguanadon, ion, ignition, injection, illustration, immersion, etc.

7. There are thousands of four-letter words.

8. Probable, proactive, probate, probe, problem, proceed, procrastinate, proctor, procure, prod, prodigious, produce, profile, progress, profit, profane, etc.

9. Backward, bard, card, forward, guard, haggard, hard, inward, laggard, leopard, regard, reward, standard, vanguard, ward, etc.

10. Old, giving bold, cold, fold, gold, hold, sold and told.

11. Eagle, earache, ease, eclipse, economise, educate, efface, elapse, elevate, elite, eloquence, elusive, elope, else, emotive, enclose, erase, estate, etc.

12. There are thousands of five-letter words.

13. Image, imagine, imbalance, imbibe, imitate, immaculate, immediate, immense, immobile, immoral, immune, imp, impact, impatient, impede, impetus, implode, imprint, improve, etc.

14. Telegram, program, hologram, anagram, monogram, epigram, diagram, parallelogram, milligram, kilogram, etc.

15. Late, giving collate, deflate, plate and slate.

16. Tarot, tint, tacit, threat, tenant, tempest, twit, text, thrift, that, thought, tent, torrent, treat, tempest, tent, test, terrorist, etc.

17. There are thousands of six-letter words.

18. Transact, transcribe, transept, transfer, transform, transgress, transistor, transit, translate, translucent, transmit, transom, transparent, transpire, transport, etc.

19. Bail, entail, fail, fantail, hail, jail, mail, nail, pail, prevail, quail, rail, retail, sail, tail, travail, wail, wassail, etc.

20. Ease, giving cease, crease, grease, lease, pease and tease.

21. Wallow, widow, willow, window, winnow, whitlow.

22. There are hundreds of seven letter words.

23. Coma, combat, combine, comb, come, combust, comet, comfort, command, comment, commercial, commit, common, compact, companion, compare, compass, complete, complex compost, etc.

24. Cable, comparable, comfortable, fable, fashionable, forgivable, immeasurable, likeable, objectionable, payable, pliable, table, sable, stable, suitable, treatable, untouchable, etc.

25. Ray, giving bray, dray, foray, fray, gray, pray, stray and tray.

26. Label, level, lethal, legal, lackadaisical, logical, local, loll, libel, liberal, lintel, literal, longitudinal, etc.

27. There are hundreds of eight-letter words.

28. Preach, preamble, precede, precinct, precious, precipice, precipitate, preclude, precocious, predator, predict, prejudice, prefect, prefer, prefix, pregnant, prehistoric, prelude, prepare, premium, present, etc.

29. Bet, bracelet, get, jennet, jet, let, meet, met, net, pet, pullet, tenet, set, skillet, sweet, turret, vet, wet, yet, etc.

30. Are, giving bare, care, dare, fare, hare, mare, pare, rare, tare and ware.

31. Nation, neuron, notion, noon, neon, neutron, newborn, nineteen, nitrogen, noggin, nocturn, nomination, nonagenarian, northern, noun, notation, nutrition, etc.

32. There are hundreds of nine-letter words.

33. Bias, bib, bible, bicarbonate, bicentennial, bicycle, bid, bidet, big, bigot, bikini, bilberry, bile, bilingual, bilious, bill, bin, binary, bind, binge, biochemistry, etc.

34. Epilogue, prologue, dialogue, travelogue, catalogue, ideologue, brogue, vogue, etc.

35. Ate, giving date, fate, gate, hate, late, mate, pate, rate and sate.

36. Radar, reader, reminder, rear, rider, remainder, rotter, ruler, rubber, rover, rotavator, raider, rotor, runner, etc.

37. There are hundreds of ten-letter words.

38. Subaltern, subcommittee, subcontinent, subcontract, subcutaneous, subframe, subject, subjugate, sublime, subliminal, submarine, submerge, submissive, subordinate, subpoena, subscribe, etc.

39. Arrogance, askance, assistance, balance, chance, dance, extravagance, lance, maintenance, nuance, penance, prance, protuberance, relevance, resemblance, séance, stance, trance, etc.

40. Oil, giving boil, broil, coil, foil, soil, spoil and toil.

YOUR SCORE

The maximum possible score is 405 words. If you scored less than 96 or more than 215 words, your results are not valid. You must have ignored the time limit, or perhaps you use letters or words professionally ... In any case, this test is not for you!

✳ 96–143 words

You're average. You have sufficient words at your disposal in order to get by on a day-to-day basis, but your poor vocabulary sometimes causes you problems.

✳ 144–173 words

You have a good knowledge of words and you are able to express yourself well; you can adapt your manner of speech to suit different people and situations.

✳ 174–215 words

You have an excellent level of vocabulary, and a remarkable capacity for expression, which, even if you are not a professional writer, makes communication easy for you.

CHAPTER 8

INCREASING YOUR SPATIAL AWARENESS

The use of intelligence assumes that one can form precise representations.

Spatial awareness is, basically, our capacity to perceive and analyse shapes. But it can, without doubt, be related to other facilities, such as 3D perception; orientation (the aptitude to recognise a form however it is presented); and visualisation (the ability to imagine how an object may move).

The following problems are designed to exercise your spatial awareness.

Give yourself 20 minutes to solve them.

TRAIN YOUR SPATIAL INTELLIGENCE

Problem 1

Find the picture that corresponds to the cuboid.

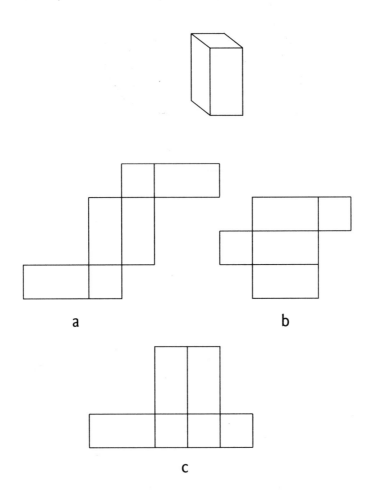

a

b

c

Problem 2

Find the number of faces of this solid.

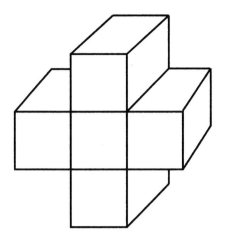

Problem 3

Group the bars according to size.

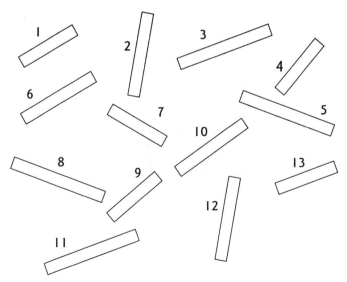

Problem 4

Group the pyramids according to their size.

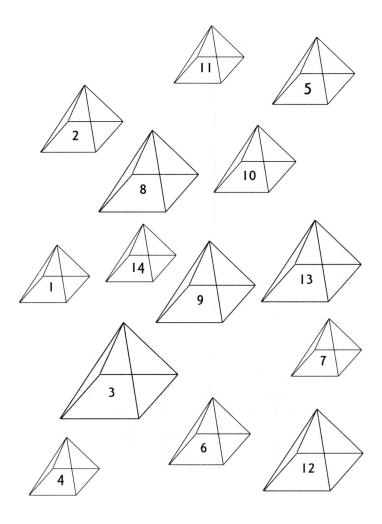

Problem 5

Find the number of elements necessary to form this parallelepiped.

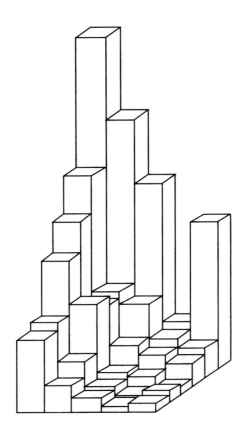

Problem 6

Find the picture that corresponds to the solid shape.

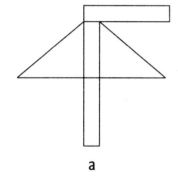

a

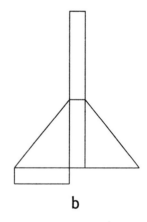

b

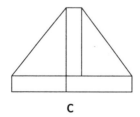

c

Problem 7

Look at the solid shape. Find its position when it is rotated through 90° clockwise.

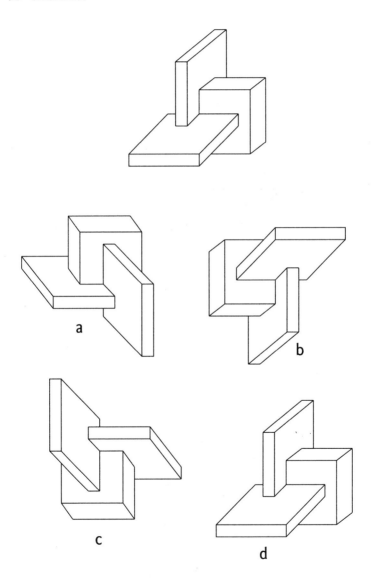

Problem 8

Find the picture that corresponds to the solid shape.

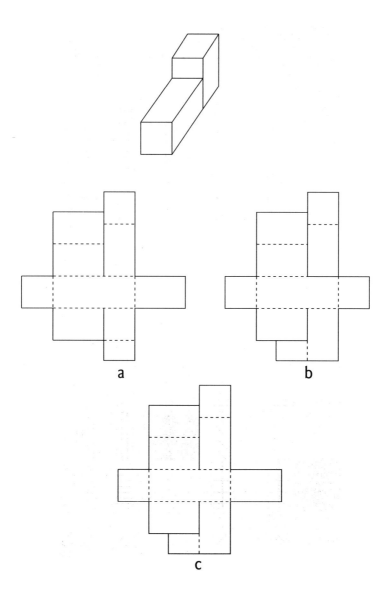

a

b

c

Problem 9

How many different designs are used for shading?

Problem 10

Look at the first diagram. Find its position when it roates through 45° to the left.

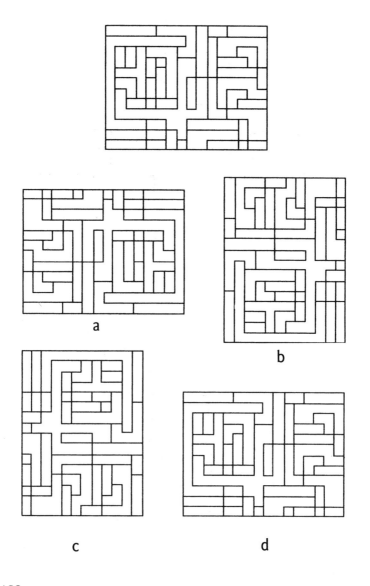

a

b

c

d

Problem 11

Find the picture that corresponds to the solid shape.

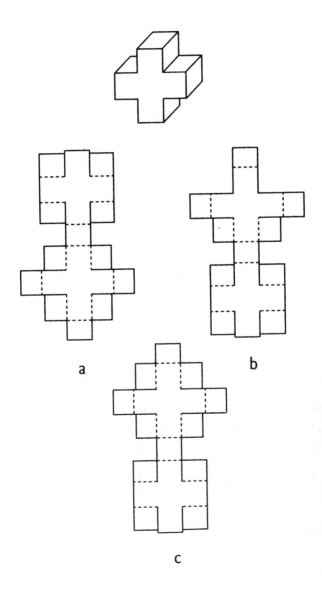

a

b

c

Problem 12

Shade in the appropriate parts of the picture to match those coloured black on the solid shape.

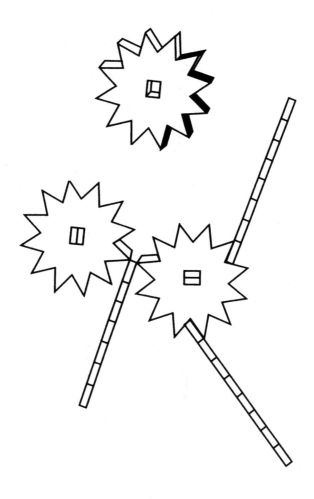

Problem 13

Look at the solid shape. Find the corresponding shape that fits into it.

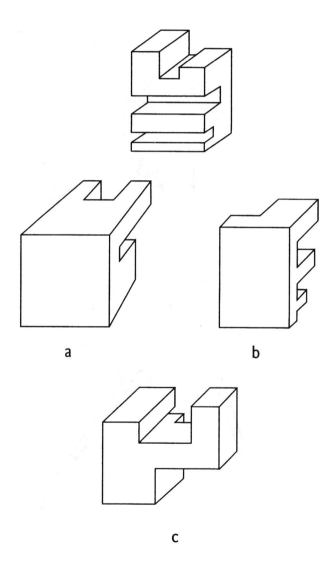

a

b

c

SOLUTIONS

1. a

2. 14

3. There are three different sizes, grouped as follows:

   1, 4, 7, 9, 13
   2, 6, 10, 12
   3, 5, 8, 11

4. There are four sizes of pyramids, grouped as follows:

   3
   8, 9, 12, 13
   2, 5, 6, 10
   1, 4, 7, 11, 14

5. 29

6. b

7. c

8. c

9. 9

10. b

11. b

12. Shade the sketch thus:

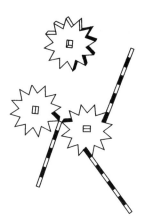

13. b

HOW TO RATE YOUR PERFORMANCE

Note: A normal total score is between 2 and 11 problems solved. If you scored above or below this, your results are not valid – you are either extraordinarily gifted or hopeless!

✳ **2–6 problems solved**

An average score. You could do with some more practice, however.

✳ **6–8 problems solved**

You have very good spatial intelligence, but you sometimes have difficulty when things are represented in different ways.

✳ **9–11 problems solved**

You have excellent powers of mental representation (or a lot of luck if you guessed your answers); you like to 'spatialise' problems in order to solve them.

We can tell more by looking at the kind of problems you solved.

✳ If you solved problems 2, 3, 4, 5 and 9, you have strong powers of spatial perception.

✳ If you solved problems 7, 10 and 13, your spatial orientation is good.

✳ If you solved problems 1, 6, 8, 11 and 12, you have good powers of visualisation.

CHAPTER 9

EMOTIONAL INTELLIGENCE

Emotional intelligence is measured by means of an emotional quotient, or EQ. A good EQ consists of two essential qualities: self-discipline and the ability to 'read' the feelings of others as well as your own. In order to stimulate your emotional intelligence, you must learn to develop these two qualities. But first of all you must evaluate your level of emotional intelligence.

TESTING YOUR EQ

On the following pages there are descriptions of 37 situations, comparable to those that Seligman designed for his recruitment tests for Metlife (see Chapter 1). In each case, choose the reply that corresponds to your most likely response.

The library fines you £5 for a book that you have not returned.

A   When I am engrossed in a book, I forget that it has to go back.

B   I was so taken up with my report that I forgot to bring it back.

You lose your temper with a friend.

A   She is always complaining.

B   She was in a bad mood.

You are penalised because you sent your tax declaration late.

A   I never pay my taxes on time.

B   I was sick of paying my taxes each year.

You feel exhausted.

A   I never take time to relax.

B   I was exceptionally busy this week.

A friend says something hurtful to you.

A   She never thinks before she speaks.

B   She was in a bad mood and so she took it out on me.

You come a cropper while skiing.

A   Skiing is difficult.

B   The piste was icy.

You put on weight during the holidays and haven't managed to lose the excess pounds.

A   Dieting is pointless.

B   The diet that I tried didn't work for me.

You accidentally break a vase at your mother-in-law's house.

A   It was an awful-looking thing anyway.

B   I'll buy her another one.

You drive through a puddle and splash a pedestrian.

A   He should not have been on the edge of the pavement.

B   I must apologise.

A friend misses his train because of you. You tell him:

A   You should not have waited for me.

B   It's my fault, I should have left sooner.

You forget to wish your friend Happy Birthday.

A   I always forget birthdays.

B   I was too busy that day to think about it.

One morning your partner doesn't kiss you before leaving.

A   They don't want to because I wasn't very nice to them yesterday evening.

B   They have an important meeting this morning.

You say some very unkind things to a friend.

A   I can't stand it when they complain all the time.

B   I was very on edge that day.

You can't lose a stone.

A   I don't understand it, I tried really hard.

B   I must be too greedy.

Your boss accuses you of being dishonest.

A   He doesn't trust anybody.

B   He must have the taxman on his back.

The friends you are waiting for are already 30 minutes late.

A   I'll give them another three minutes then I'm going.

B   They must have been caught in the traffic.

An old lady bumps into you in the street.

A   Old people think they can get away with anything.

B   I should have been watching where I was going.

In the car, your partner takes the wrong road.

A   I could have told you it was the other way.

B   It doesn't matter, it'll only mean a short detour.

In a shop, a sales assistant tells you that she doesn't have any more of the trousers that you want in your size.

A   They never have what I want.

B   I shouldn't have waited for the sales.

Your partner reproaches you for not being very loving with them.

A   They never really do anything to deserve it.

B   I just wasn't thinking.

For several days, your child has moaned every morning before leaving for school.

A   How I could have produced such a pathetic child?

B   I wonder if he has a problem with his classmates.

A friend cancels dinner at the last minute.

A   I could never count on them.

B   They couldn't help it.

Your partner questions your fidelity.

A   They are jealous of everyone.

B   I provoked them a bit.

A work colleague bursts into tears at the office.

A   She does it to draw attention to herself.

B   She must have a problem at home.

Christmas is:

A   Just an excuse to get presents.

B   A time of goodwill, especially for children.

Your mother-in-law invites herself for Sunday lunch (again). You refuse, on the grounds that:

A   She shouldn't expect to make a habit of it.

B   You have a prior engagement.

A policeman stops you for going through a red light. You tell him:

A   I didn't, the light wasn't even orange.

B   I'm sorry, I wasn't aware of it.

Your best love letter is:

A   The one that I never sent.

B   The first one I received.

On days when there is a full moon:

A   I really don't feel any difference.

B   I am not at all my normal self.

You are faced with spending a day without seeing anyone.

A   I'll make the best of it by sorting out my papers and correspondence.

B   It gives me time for myself.

As a couple, you should:

A   Be able to go to dinner with an ex without it causing a big drama.

B   Each have your own hobbies.

When your friends talk about their jobs you sometimes envy them because:

A   They don't have worries to trouble themselves with.

B   They have a family life too.

You would like to be able to change your job to get:

A   A bigger office.

B   More exciting work.

The best way to stay healthy is:

A   To take care of yourself all the time.

B   To feel good about your body.

When your boss tells you off:

A   I tell him a few home truths.

B   I walk out and wait for him to calm down.

True love:

A   Is often an illusion.

B   Is gradually built by the two of you together.

On your keyring there are:

A   Only keys.

B   At least one good luck charm.

YOUR SCORE

The more **A**s you scored, the more likely you are to have a low EQ. Your lack of emotional intelligence is probably dragging you down.

However, if you scored a high number of **A**s (more than 19), don't panic. Emotional intelligence is complex, by definition. It combines numerous different and often elusive qualities, such as self-awareness, consistency, tact and empathy, the ability to identify with others and feel what they feel. You cannot quantify it as you can an IQ; you can only evaluate it as a tendency towards particular feelings or behaviour. Also, EQ is not fixed at birth. If you think you may have a weak EQ, there are things you can do. In the next three chapters I shall tell you what you can do to improve your EQ.

CHAPTER 10

STRENGTHENING YOUR SELF-CONTROL

It's often believed that exercising self-control means suppressing emotions. This is not so. Controlling your emotions doesn't, for example, prevent you from flying into a rage. Rather the opposite, in fact, except that you don't do it with just anybody, anywhere, anyhow, but with the right person, at the right moment, for the right reasons and to the right degree.

First of all, self-control is a question of measuring out emotions. If we often find it very difficult to react appropriately, that is because our brain is working on two different levels at the same time: one emotional and the other logical.

Pieces of information that we receive from outside ourselves are conveyed first of all by our emotional mind before passing into our rational, logical mind. This includes everything from declarations of love, compliments and criticisms to the thought of that little dress or car that you would give anything to have. And sometimes they may 'blow a fuse' in your mind so that you can't resist that box of chocolates or bottle of whisky, even though you know that it will give you a hellish migraine; or you slam out of your boss's office just because they make an unfortunate remark. You have to learn to train yourself to remain cool and optimistic. And to achieve this, there are different methods that you can employ on a daily basis.

REPROGRAMME YOUR OUTLOOK

We all suffer to some extent from what the experts call 'negative programming'. This is created by negative messages received during infancy that come from parents, teachers and other children. And these negative messages can be reactivated when we are treated unfavourably in some way. As adults, we are frequently subjected to reproach and criticism in our professional and private lives. These negative messages influence our self-esteem and morale, even when we have good reason to be proud of ourselves.

Furthermore, in a world where self-image is important, it is easy to feel low if we compare ourselves to, public figures as they are portrayed in the media.

All this means that we often view the world in a negative way. We say to ourselves: 'I must...', 'I shouldn't...', 'I'm always having to...'. But we can reprogramme ourselves to react positively. This simply means always seeing the good side of things – because there always is one. And it's a course of action that's easy to adopt. Of course we all have to work within the constraints of our professional and personal lives, but you will strengthen and reinforce your self-control if you remember to say 'I can...', 'I want...', 'I've decided that...', instead of your previous responses.

There's an old story that has been told many times in the great schools of American commerce. It concerns two shoe retailers' representatives who were sent to investigate sales prospects on an island in the Pacific. The first one wired home: 'Bad news, the natives aren't wearing shoes.' The second: 'Good news, the natives aren't wearing shoes.' It's all a question of being optimistic and looking for the bright side of situations.

CONNECT WITH YOUR RIGHT HEMISPHERE

The brain functions with an alternating current. The left hemisphere is logical, sensible, realistic and 'pessimistic' by nature; the right is intuitive, creative and optimistic. In the normal course of events, we keep moving from one to the other and all goes well.

If you are constantly chewing things over in your mind, feeling morose and defeatist, it's because you have become blocked in the left side of your brain. In order to reinforce your self-control, you must connect with your right brain once more. The trick is something like counting sheep when you can't sleep – in this case you replace the words that are churning around in your head with images. You are, in effect, using self-hypnosis from time to time in order to clear your head.

The process is quite simple. Focus your attention on an object or a light-coloured surface and count to 20 very slowly. When you get to 20, close your eyes and for 10 minutes visualise the object or the surface that you were looking at. Keep telling yourself that, while this is going on, it is impossible to open your eyes. At the end of the 10 minutes, when you open your eyes, you will feel like a new person!

However, for the process to work, you must believe in it. Scepticism is controlled by the left hemisphere of the brain. Eventually, with practice and confidence, you will be able to branch voluntarily into the right side of your brain simply by closing your eyes.

STOP THE WORLD

Your mind also has a capacity for 'auto-intoxication'. Too much worry, overwork or stress will automatically put the brain into a state of under- or overactivity. As a result, the mechanism of your mind either jams or goes into overdrive. You find that you're unable to think straight or you're completely down in the dumps; either way, this reduces your self-control.

In order to clear your mind and boost your morale once more, you must learn to 'stop the world'. There are several ways of doing this. You can take frequent short breaks, close your eyes for several seconds or minutes during the day, to block out the tide of information and simply empty your head.

Of course, at first your thoughts will continue to churn around. Try to detach yourself from them; relax, let your mind drift out of your body, let your thoughts flow freely, watch them as they move around, without concentrating on them.

By becoming a mere spectator of your own thoughts, you relax your mental state. Now, if a problem is bothering you, imagine that you are putting it in a box. Then you can tidy away the box in a safe place until you are able to solve the problem. Afterwards, dig a hole to bury it in for good, or throw it into the sea.

With a bit of practice, you will find it quite easy to stand back from your worries and troubles, to stop the world whenever it gets too much or when you are out of sorts.

GIVE YOUR BRAIN TIME OUT

This consists of altering your reactions to give your brain time to read your feelings, adjust to a situation and take it in hand. These techniques are well known to and used by many professional actors, top-class athletes and even bomb disposal experts.

* Expand your solar plexus (where the ribs join at the bottom of your chest), pull back your shoulders and hold in your stomach. Breathe in deeply and hold your breath for two seconds. Then exhale and wait for two seconds before breathing in again.

* Close your eyes for two or three seconds from time to time. By blocking out everything you see, you ease the pressure on your emotional brain which leaves you time to install information into your logical brain. You can do it in the street, at your desk, in a meeting (nobody will notice), but don't try doing it when you are behind the wheel!

* Open your mouth wide for one or two seconds from time to time. This activates the muscles that encase the cranial nerves and allows them to ease the pressure on the brain.

Try to do all these exercises several times a day. At first they may seem a bit tedious but soon you will feel so much better in yourself, more in touch with your feelings, more flexible in your relationships with others, that your brain will no longer be able to do without them. Using them will become automatic.

LEARNING HOW TO LET GO

We all have to make concessions and compromises at times. However, we don't always do it as quickly or as often as we should. We tend to hang on to things in order to protect our pride, our rights and our territory. Some people will fight ferociously in order to defend their family, their traditions or their property, preferring to suffer or even die rather than accept defeat.

This reflex emerges at all levels in our daily lives. It comes into play when we are emotionally involved, so we cling to love even when it is already dead, and we hold on to a job even when it is not right for us. But it can also make us hang on to silly things that we don't really care about. For instance, there's that man in a telephone box, just finishing his conversation. He goes to hang up. You approach, a little too quickly, because you also need to use the telephone – and he starts up the conversation again. He is holding on to what he has, probably without even realising what he's doing.

The same thing happens in a discussion. It often takes only one person to disagree to make all the others dig their heels in. Sometimes we prefer to get angry rather than turn the other cheek. We know, deep down, we don't really give a damn one way or the other and yet we hold on instinctively, and also out of pride. Buoyed up by our own self-justification, we may, quite often, deliberately make ourselves angry and upset a perfectly happy relationship.

Of course it's annoying when someone barges in when you're waiting in a queue. But you will feel less upset if you just let things go, and avoid confrontation. Equally, it's aggravating when your partner throws tantrums like a spoilt child. But it will be less stressful if you don't make a scene too. So learn to hold yourself back and let things go. This new approach to life requires that you follow several rules.

Rule 1: Do only what you want to do; be guided by your feelings.

If you don't want to conform, steer clear of groups and partnerships. You are not obliged to do what everybody else does. When you do something, do it for yourself, not because of pressure from other people. Similarly, if you are not interested in playing the piano or jogging, don't do it. Let it go. Don't give yourself a hard time under the pretext of it being chic, fashionable or good for your health. You must have other talents elsewhere that are less of a drag and come more naturally to you.

Make choices you like, do things you enjoy – otherwise they will be ill-judged and probably badly done. Listen to your feelings and your intuition. Be flexible, go with the flow. Don't try to force things – it never works. Whether it is love, promotion or any other kind of advantage you seek, fighting and grabbing are not reliable ways to get what you want. Also, prizes tend to be harder to keep than to win: the longer you have them, the more anxious you may become at the idea of losing them and the more stressed you will be in your efforts to hold on to them.

Rule 2: Detach yourself when problems arise.

First of all, restrict all areas of conflict. You probably already have enough problems without creating others. So, you must get out of difficult relationships as quickly as possible and choose your friends carefully. Surround yourself with people with whom you share the same values, the same ideas or the same lifestyle. This makes things easier, as there will be fewer reasons for disagreement so arguments will be less frequent and will blow over quickly.

Even with those closest to you (or perhaps especially with them), you must avoid confrontation. Remember the old adage: 'Don't talk politics or religion at the table'. Don't defend your territory or your point of view at any price. If your ideas or your plans aren't acceptable to your friends, drop them – at least for the time being. If your lifestyle or your habits don't please, take them elsewhere. Whether a relationship is one of love or just friendship, it should feel natural. And if rows do occur, the end result must be worth the unpleasantness.

Of course, once you are away from home, in your job for example, you often have no choice but to put up with things as they are. But the principle remains the same: be prepared to step back or stand down in order to avoid souring a situation or relationship. Be as vague as is necessary – you can keep your true thoughts and objectives safe in your head, ready to be brought out at a more opportune moment.

You will find that the majority of your problems will sort themselves out if you don't make a issue of them. In a suprisingly short time, people calm down, get things into perspective and find some grounds for compromise – or even agreement.

Rule 3: Don't turn everything into a personal problem.

When you have a row with someone you are probably quite unaware of what is going on inside their head. If they appear unnecessarily moody or critical you are quite likely to fly off the handle or flounce off in a rage. What may not occur to you is that they may have problems of their own.

Usually when you have a disagreement with someone at the office or at home, it's over something very minor. You may get the brunt of it simply because you have the bad luck to be in the wrong place at the wrong time and it's always disagreeable to get the rough end of someone else's temper. But you can hardly reproach others for what you sometimes do yourself. So try to remember that everyone has the right to be in a bad mood occasionally; everyone has the odd off day. Don't let things get to you. Step back from the situation. Train yourself to ignore it and concentrate your attention on other things. By not reacting, by remaining emotionally detached, you will nip the situation in the bud and stop it from developing into something worse.

Rule 4: Don't be judgmental.

It's very tempting to judge other people. When you are in the right, it's hard to resist driving the other person into a corner. You take pleasure in pointing out their weaknesses and their mistakes. You are so busy being right, and enjoying your position on the high moral ground, that you forget that anyone – even you – can slip up.

Letting go is also learning to be more tolerant. We must be prepared to acknowledge that not everyone thinks or acts in the same way; there are different ways and they are all equally valid. We should not expect or try to exert our own authority on every situation or person we meet.

CHAPTER 11

LEARNING TO READ YOUR FEELINGS

Good self-control is essential in order to leave time for your sensible brain to register what you feel at any given moment. It's a bit like the pause when a computer loads a program before showing a response on the screen. But there's more to it than that.

The problem with feelings is that we often make mistakes. We imagine feelings that we don't have. For instance, we say, 'I hate So-and-so'. But we don't actually mean it. We may not like him because of something he has said or done, but it is unlikely to amount to real hatred.

In the same way, we deny feelings that we do have. We say, 'I couldn't give a damn that What's-her-name won't co-operate with me at work'. But we really want What's-her-name to like us a bit. When you share an office for seven or eight hours a day, it creates bonds, whether you like it or not.

If you want to learn how to understand yourself, you could take yourself to a therapist three times a week, but there are simpler and cheaper ways.

DEPROGRAMME YOURSELF

When we misinterpret feelings, it's often because the words we use to describe them are inappropriate. For example, we say to ourselves 'I noticed it too late', 'It's not a good time', 'I can't do it', 'I didn't hear anything', 'I haven't got time', 'I don't want to make waves' and so on. But it's all a load of rubbish – these are just excuses that we make up to protect ourselves while continuing to tell ourselves that we're being honest with other people. The truth is that we're restricted by our own circumstances – we are, if you like, pre-programmed so that we misinterpret our own feelings.

We do this for all sorts of reasons. As adults, we are all holding inside us the warnings and scoldings we received as children. These rise to the surface of our minds each time that we are confronted by something new. So, when challenged by an unknown situation, a voice in our heads says, 'You are going to look stupid', or ' You're not going to make it', etc. We all have mental commands programmed in our brain, which limit our potential and may even prevent us from establishing relationships. They form invisible and impassable barriers between us and our own feelings and other people.

There are five mental commands embedded in our minds, each corresponding to a reprimand that we used to receive from our parents. Each one arouses associated feelings in us, which we may not even realise are there.

Be strong

Associated feeling: pride. This makes you hold back so that you seem a bit distant, almost disdainful. You may not want to show your feelings; you don't enjoy being paid compliments. You feel unappreciated and prefer to remain detached from others rather than risk putting yourself in a situation where you could be rejected.

Hurry up

Associated feeling: distress. This makes you complain a lot; you sulk; you don't listen, you talk incessantly. You feel as though you are in a permanent state of emergency. You are always trying to do the maximum amount in record time. You don't take the time to examine your feelings because if you did you would run the risk of calling into question many things in your life.

Be nice

Associated feeling: inferiority. Deep down you don't feel you have any talent, you doubt yourself and your potential. You stick rigidly to your habits and find it difficult to fit in with other people. You shut off your own feelings so that you don't have to look too closely at your own opinions and values.

Don't argue

Associated feelings: fear and timidity. You force yourself to be nice to everyone, to put yourself in a good light. In your efforts to smooth over difficult situations, you say 'Yes' even when you're thinking 'No!'. You pretend to feel things you don't, to avoid being out of step with other people.

Make an effort

Associated feeling: guilt. You don't believe in yourself; you are scared of making a mistake; you let opportunities pass you by, telling yourself that this isn't the right time. You don't see relationships through. You deny feelings to avoid being punished if things go wrong ('I might let her down', 'He's going to want something from me', 'They'll hold it against me', and so on).

TAKE RESPONSIBILITY FOR YOUR OWN FEELINGS

It is important to remember that about 75 per cent of what we say goes unnoticed, is misunderstood or is immediately forgotten.

Given these circumstances, we need to follow some basic rules if we are going to get emotional about things. After all, there are some risks involved: displays of emotion are often taken as a sign of weakness and may all too easily lead to mistakes and misunderstandings.

Recognise your rights (and those of other people)

You are entitled to have contradicting emotions and feelings and to express them, provided that the time and the place are appropriate.

You don't have to appreciate or approve of the attitude or behaviour of somebody just because you live or work with them. You are allowed to express your own opinions and values, provided that, in doing so, you don't hurt or belittle anyone.

You have the right to talk about your problems. When you ask someone to listen to you, make it clear that you want to talk now.

You are entitled to say 'Yes' or 'No' as you please. So don't say 'Yes' just for the sake of agreement if you don't really agree or if it doesn't please you.

You are allowed to be weak. Don't cover yourself in excuses when you've made a mistake or if you have failed to come up to expectations. Don't drag yourself in the mud.

You have the right to change your opinion. It is stupid to stick to your guns and fence yourself in during an argument when you know you are wrong.

You don't have to accept everything just because someone says so. Learn to say 'I don't know', 'I don't understand' or 'I don't agree'. Learn to use these phrases whenever you don't feel at ease or when something displeases you.

Always speak up if you feel uncomfortable about something. Don't keep your doubts or negative feelings to yourself.

You are allowed to keep some space and some time for yourself. Even if you share everything with someone, you must always have your own territory. The right to feelings is also the right to be alone, to enjoy silence and tranquillity. The majority of arguments between couples happen when they meet up again after work. One comes home with their problems and throws them in the other's face without stopping to consider that they may also have their own worries. Take the time to unwind. Don't impose on others and don't let them impose on you.

Learn to listen to others

Feelings are fragile and are easily hurt by words. Avoid saying any of the following:

Sort it out yourself – you're driving me mad.

You should go and see a psychiatrist.

Stop that stupid crying. I can't stand it when you get in a state.

You know what's wrong with you, you always make a big deal out of things.

Make an effort.

Why should I make an effort if you don't?

It's your fault.

Bully for you.

I've already told you.

I warned you this would happen.

Learn to listen properly: that means listening without criticising, neither judging nor condemning (especially when you don't agree). Take note of the feelings and problems of the other person. It is worth making the effort: listening to someone else's problems will help to take you out of yourself.

Get in touch with your dreams

Our dreams are the true representation of our feelings. If your EQ is rather low, you probably don't dream much but, theoretically, you can dream on command.

Learning to dream, being in charge of your thoughts, is a traditional practice amongst many ancient tribes and religions. In recent years, there has been much laboratory experimentation into dreams and dreaming. In America, Stephen Laberge, Professor of Psychophysiology at Stanford University, has even invented the idea of 'lucid dreaming'. His technique consists of using a pair of glasses linked up to a computer to detect the smallest dream activity through eye movements. Learning to dream to order takes a great deal of time and training. On the other hand, it's quite simple to learn how to dream.

First of all, you need to be in the right physical condition.

❋ Do not have a heavy meal on the evening that you wish to 'programme' a dream. Drink only water. Alcohol induces sleep too quickly. Also avoid tea and coffee after lunchtime.

❋ Avoid intense physical or intellectual effort before you go to bed. Don't go for a jog or do a workout on this evening, and don't read anything too heavy.

❋ Make yourself comfortable in bed so you are as calm as possible. Lie on your back with your head quite low (avoid big pillows). Have the room as quiet as possible – noise will disturb both sleep and dreams.

Avoid falling into a deep sleep instantly. Normally, sleep is preceded by a phase of falling asleep that lasts for several minutes. During this phase, mental activity involves visual and auditory hallucinations. You need to benefit from this moment in order to prepare yourself for dreaming. All the images that form while you are falling asleep automatically reappear in your dreams, albeit in an incomplete or distorted form.

Finally, visualise the dream that you would like to have.

❋ Start by relaxing yourself, emptying your head of thoughts. Let your mind wander as it wishes. Don't dwell on your problems or your worries, just let them flow through your mind.

✳ Now imagine a scene. Firstly the person or the setting (start with whichever is easier for you). You must form a perfect image of each as if you are watching a private slide show. Put the finishing touches to it, concentrate on the texture of skin, the glow of a light. As soon as you have done this, go on to the next stage.

✳ Now you can make up your own scenario. First of all focus on the climax of your dream, your dominant feeling in this situation. Apprehension, excitement, tenderness, etc., try to 'preview' each movement, each gesture, of yourself and of others. How easily you visualise them depends on your degree of perception, and also the types of sensations that you associate with them.

Ideally, you should spend at least 10 minutes in this state, suspended between dreaming and reality. The first few times, before you become proficient, you will probably fall asleep too quickly. But, with practice, you will be able to achieve this without any problem. Your first dream can then start. This is usually an hour to an hour and a half after you went to sleep.

Make yourself take the trouble to write down your dream each time. Note, in brief detail, the people, the situations, the settings, and also your impressions. Describe everything that you experienced. You will soon find that you dream more often and that you remember your dreams more easily; you will also feel more in touch with your real feelings.

GETTING THE RIGHT VIEWPOINT

When you read your own feelings, you are at the same time both the object and the subject of your observations. You see yourself, but what you see is influenced by your way of looking at yourself. Any progress will depend, above all, on your state of mind. Being able to 'connect' with your feelings means taking the right attitude. The following principles are essential for the success of your meditation. They can also help you to make life easier for yourself every day.

❋ Don't wait for things to happen. Act on, and take, initiatives without worrying about the results. You will do things better.

❋ Don't fight to get things. It is important to be consistent in your efforts and if you have to fight to obtain things, you will inevitably be forced to fight to keep them.

❋ Take your time. It always takes time to achieve worthwhile objectives.

❋ Learn to let go. Don't get overattached to anything but don't reject things out of hand either. You will find it easier to face the ups and downs in your life if you learn to take a more casual attitude to things.

❋ Accept yourself just as you are. You will quickly shake off your faults and weaknesses once you stop putting yourself down.

❋ Be nice to yourself. You may not be perfect, but you're all you've got!

❋ Be pragmatic. Avoid forming preconceived ideas about other people and events. Forget your prejudices and wait and see for yourself.

❋ Treat all your problems as opportunities. Everything that appears negative to you can help you to develop and grow.

❋ Avoid worry. You don't need to rationalise or calculate everything. Learn to trust your sensitivity and your intuition.

❋ Don't keep comparing yourself to others. It only creates problems. If you think you are not as good as someone else you will feel embarrassed or ashamed and probably become jealous. And if you think you are better than the others, you will appear scornful and proud.

CHAPTER 12

LEARNING TO READ THE FEELINGS OF OTHERS

We frequently get stuck in a rut with our partners, our family or our job because we don't know how to communicate with others very well, if at all. Normally, 90 per cent of all communication is non-verbal, through our emotions. It depends on our ability to 'read' other people's feelings.

Robert Rosenthal, a psychologist from Harvard, has shown that our EQ is linked to our ability to read emotional signals. He has tested this using a silent film where a young lady expresses different feelings: anger, love, jealousy, gratitude and charm. Sometimes only her head is visible, and sometimes her eyes are closed, so that her emotions have to be identified using only subtle signals. Adults who score highly in this test have been discovered to have higher rates of success in their jobs and with their relationships. Children who scored highly in the test were also found to be popular at school and scored well academically, even if they had only a fairly average IQ.

However, it is no good simply resolving to pay more attention to people in order to develop this ability. You will find that although this works to start with, you will soon fall back into your old habits. You must instead use more effective methods to improve your ability to communicate with others.

STIMULATE YOUR VISUAL MEMORY

Everything that passes into our visual field is registered in our brain. By stimulating certain parts of the brain with electrodes, it is possible to recreate a person's whole life, so that they can accurately describe all the millions of people they have seen from the moment they first opened their eyes. However, if someone asks you what your boss or loved one was wearing yesterday, you would probably be unable to answer!

Paying attention to others starts in the visual memory. We must stimulate it in order to be better at reading other people's feelings.

Every time that you meet someone new, take a mental note of all their particulars, the clothes that they are wearing as well as the way they stand, their way of walking, their verbal mannerisms, etc. When you get home, try to remember all these little details and write them down.

Soon this will become second nature and you will also discover that you find it easier to read others' feelings and emotions.

SEPARATE IMAGE FROM SOUND

Try watching the television with the sound turned down. You will be lost at first. You won't understand what is happening, you can't follow it. But after a while, you will become much more sensitive to subtle body language, movements, faces and expressions. This is because, instead of being influenced by the sounds people make, and the reactions they produce in your emotions, you are concentrating on a rational appraisal of what is actually represented in front of you.

BE MORE REALISTIC

Often we don't know how to read other people's feelings because we don't see them as they are. Instead, we want to change people or things to fit the situation as we think it should, ideally, be. But this may not always be possible. So you should try to be more realistic, and not overestimate your own 'power'.

In life there are situations, events and people whom you cannot either support or fight against. If you are dealing with a person who does not wish to communicate with you, all the goodwill and encouragement in the world are ineffective. You are wasting your time attempting to convince a committed racist that a multi-racial society is an attractive prospect, or a manic depressive that they can snap out of their misery simply by making an effort. You will only end up by discouraging yourself, and losing confidence in your own ability to make yourself understood. You will test your patience to the limits and may very well also end up doubting the humanity of those around you.

So accept others as they are. Concentrate on looking after yourself first and you will avoid misleading yourself. Accept that there are good reasons why relationships either work or break up. Learn to take into account your feelings as well as those of the other person.

DON'T TRY TO ARGUE AGAINST PREJUDICE

Thankfully, we don't all think the same. Beliefs, like tastes and colours, are all different. An opinion of any sort (Margaret Thatcher was a good prime minister, white bread is bad for your health...) always has an emotional or irrational dimension to it. If you try to prove to someone that their view is wrong, you will, as often as not, only strengthen their prejudices. Suppose you come across a tribe of people who believe that the earth is flat. In order to demonstrate the contrary to them, you show them satellite photos. They will, in all likelihood, react by asserting that the photographs are false, made-up or fixed.

If you are going to take other people's feelings into account, you also have to make way for their prejudices. You will have to be prepared to·compromise if you are going to communicate effectively. After all, if you think about it, you probably already do this with your friends. You make allowances for their prejudices (just as they accommodate yours). Or, you simply avoid subjects on which you find their opinions unacceptable. Finally, don't ever try to argue with fanatics or fundamentalists of any kind.

REFUSE TO BE FORCED INTO ANY RELATIONSHIP

In a forced relationship, there is no room for feelings on the part of either of the participants. So, just as you would never dream of accepting an invitation to box with Mike Tyson, don't ever let yourself be forced into anything, whether it is at work, in the street or even at home. In a forced relationship, there is always a loser. Even if you are the one who comes out on top, it's only ever a superficial victory: there will be unresolved, underlying problems and one day they will resurface, often in a more vicious form.

You can clearly see when a relationship is being forced on you. You find yourself giving in because you have no choice; you feel that by surrendering you are sacrificing your own feelings and interests. You may think you have resigned yourself to the situation, but you will never be happy with it. You brood over the injustice of it and dream of being able to take revenge.

IGNORE AGGRESSIVE BEHAVIOUR

Aggression is another thing that cuts us off from other people's feelings. It may be direct aggression, through threats and insults, or indirect, using innuendo or subtle, hurtful suggestions. Any kind of attack is deeply disturbing. Your aggressor takes you by surprise. The violence or ambiguity of what they imply makes your blood boil. Shocked by the violent emotion, you are either left speechless or provoked into an equally aggressive reaction. If you know you are going to be confronted by this sort of thing at the office each day, you will feel less than enthusiastic about going to work (unless, of course, you are an adrenaline junkie). And if it's happening in a relationship, it's even worse.

The best course of action is always to refuse to acknowledge such attacks. This gives you the time to regain your equilibrium, analyse the reasons for the aggression and prepare a good response. So if the attack is brutal, walk away. By breaking contact, you cut the attack short and, whenever possible, you should avoid fuelling it further. This is not cowardice: rather, it allows you to retake the initiative in the relationship and gives you the chance to smooth things over.

AVOID INSINCERITY

An insincere person is one who traps you, leading you to believe in feelings that they don't have, by lying deliberately to you, or by fooling themselves.

In such a case, the relationship is impossible in either the short or the long term, for it is distorted from the start. Your arguments are blocked or, worse, turned against you. You will try in vain to sell an idea or a project, to defend your point of view or your convictions, to express your own feelings.

It is easy to recognise insincere people. Anyone who is openly cynical, or makes frequent use of irony is bad news. People who badmouth all their friends behind their backs, or who are always criticising everything, or gushing all over you are no better. Anyone who sees problems everywhere; people who are suspicious of everything; pessimists; people who can't – and won't – change their views; people who always have something to complain about (whether it's bad luck, death, being misunderstood, or just the sheer spitefulness of other people) – they are all in some way insincere.

BE MORE SELFISH

Every day you make sacrifices. You give up your pleasures and put aside personal interests. Most of the time this is not very important. It's not a big deal if you don't buy that Armani outfit that's just made for you because your child needs a new jacket. It doesn't matter if you give up going out with your friends because your partner is in bed with the flu. It's not a tragedy if you feel you must agree to spend a weekend at a health farm with your mother, although you know that three days with her will drive you up the wall.

But sometimes you find you are giving up more essential things. You may compromise your personal individuality just to conform better to the image that other people have of you. Or perhaps you give up a hobby, or a project, or even a long-held dream in order to fit better into a the role that is expected of you. Or you stay with a partner that you no longer love because you have had children together and you think that keeping up the appearance of being a family will be better than the reality of a divorce.

It probably seems that every time you have to make a sacrifice you can justify the pain it will cause you. You justify it by appealing to your own finer feelings. You 'owe' it to your mother, your friend, your partner or your children. But you are deceiving yourself. Who are you to think you know what is best for other people? Maybe your child doesn't need a new coat as much as he needs parents who are happy in themselves. Maybe if your mother was left alone for that weekend at the health farm, she would meet new friends to brighten up her old age. And maybe a few days without you would do a world of good to the person who shares your life.

After all, it is possible to be selfish without upsetting other people. It may mean sending other people off to deal with their own problems, instead of constantly running after them yourself, but it will allow you to take both your own feelings and those of others into account more effectively. And that is one of the hallmarks of true emotional intelligence.